workskills™

Situational Judgment
and Active Listening

workskills™

Situational Judgment
and Active Listening

PROGRAM CONSULTANTS

Bonnie Goonen

Susan Pittman-Shetler

Steck-Vaughn®

HOUGHTON MIFFLIN HARCOURT

www.steckvaughn.com/adulted
800-289-4490

Photo Acknowledgements:
P. cover ©Tim Pannell/Corbis; 4 (tl), 16–17 ©Andersen Ross/Getty Images; 5© Siede Preis/Photodisc/Getty Images; 40–41 ©Comstock/Getty Images; 4 (c), 62–63 ©Newstock/Alamy; 90–91 ©Ryan McVay/Photodisc; 4 (bl), 128–129 ©Rayman/Getty Images.

Printed in the U.S.A.

ISBN 978-0-547-53655-2

3 4 5 6 7 8 9 10 1689   20 19 18 17 16 15 14 13 12 11

4500298569   A B C D E F G

Table of Contents

Welcome to Steck-Vaughn's *WorkSkills*™   6

Pretest Assessment (Online)   🖱

Chapter 1   **Solve Problems and Make Decisions**

    Lesson 1: Problem Solving: The First Steps   18

    Lesson 2: Problem Solving: Look for Solutions   26

    Skills for the Workplace: Signs in the Workplace   34

    Chapter 1 Assessment 🖱   36

Chapter 2   **Active Listening**

    Lesson 3: Purpose for Active Listening 🎧   42

    Lesson 4: Strategies for Active Listening 🎧   50

    Skills for the Workplace: Body Language   58

    Chapter 2 Assessment 🖱   60

Chapter 3   **Resolve Conflict**

    Lesson 5: Recognize and Acknowledge Conflict 🎧   64

    Lesson 6: Resolve Conflict 🎧   74

    Skills for the Workplace: Recognize Barriers   84

    Chapter 3 Assessment 🖱   86

Chapter 4   **Cooperate with Others**

    Lesson 7: Key Skills for Cooperation in the Workplace 🎧 92

    Lesson 8: Work as Part of a Team—Personal 🎧   102

    Lesson 9: Work as Part of a Team—Interpersonal 🎧   112

    Skills for the Workplace: Social Skills   122

    Chapter 4 Assessment 🖱   124

Chapter 5   **Take Responsibility for Learning**

    Lesson 10: Get the Job Done 🎧   130

    Lesson 11: Take Initiative in the Workplace 🎧   140

    Skills for the Workplace: Inferences   150

    Chapter 5 Assessment 🖱   152

OFFICIAL Work Readiness Practice Test (Online)   🖱

***WorkSkills*™ Glossary**   156

Answers and Explanations   158

🖱 = Online Assessments

🎧 = Active Listening Scenarios

Welcome to Steck-Vaughn's *WorkSkills*™

Setting Yourself Apart in Today's Job Market

You probably already know that finding the right job for you can be a time-consuming and sometimes difficult process. You may have to sort through hundreds of job listings in order to find the few that seem right for your skills and experience.

The same is true for employers. A manager may receive hundreds or even thousands of applications for only a few open positions. How can you make yourself stand out as one of the best applicants for the job?

When looking for entry-level workers, employers want to be assured that a new employee has the knowledge and skills that he or she needs in order to be successful. Many of the skills that can help you stand out to a potential employer are also skills that you use every day. Have you ever:

- read or written an e-mail?

- estimated whether you had enough money to buy something?

- resolved a conflict with a friend or family member?

- spoken with a technical support person to solve a problem with your cell phone or computer?

If so, then you have used skills that employers value and that will help you succeed in finding and keeping a job.

Steck-Vaughn's *WorkSkills*™ is designed to assist you in identifying these skills and **developing your strengths** in these areas. Together with the **National Work Readiness Credential,** *WorkSkills*™ helps you to prove to potential employers that **you are ready for a great career!**

What Can the National Work Readiness Credential Do for You?

Some skills are specific to a particular job. If you work in construction, you probably don't need to know how to operate a cash register. However, there are other skills that apply to almost every job. The National Work Readiness Council has worked with employers in many fields to identify the knowledge, skills, and abilities needed by entry-level employees. These skills fall into four main categories:

- **Communication Skills:** reading with understanding, listening actively, speaking clearly, and thinking critically

- **Interpersonal Skills:** cooperating with others, negotiating, resolving conflicts, and giving and receiving support

- **Decision-Making Skills:** identifying and solving problems (including some that require math), making decisions, and planning ahead

- **Lifelong Learning Skills:** taking responsibility for your own learning, identifying your strengths and weaknesses, and being willing and motivated to learn new skills

Earning the National Work Readiness Credential shows employers that you have these skills. It also shows that you are motivated, have a strong work ethic, and are willing to take initiative. These qualities will set you apart from many other people who are applying for the same jobs that you are. The National Work Readiness Credential gives you an edge by showing employers that you have what it takes to succeed on the job.

To earn the National Work Readiness Credential, you will need to take and pass four separate tests:

- **Reading**
- **Math**
- **Situational Judgment**
- **Active Listening**

Prove Your Potential with *WorkSkills*™

The *WorkSkills*™ series is designed to provide you with the instruction and practice you need to master the National Work Readiness Credential assessment. This series will help you make progress toward your career goals. The *WorkSkills*™ books focus on applying reading, math, listening and speaking, and interpersonal skills in real-world workplace scenarios. In these books, all of the skills and strategies you learn will be taught in the context of real workplace scenarios, the kinds of situations that you will encounter on the job. Each lesson will teach the strategy, show you how to apply it, and then give you lots of examples that allow you to practice applying the skill or strategy to real workplace situations.

Consistent Lesson Structure Enhances Mastery

Every lesson in the *WorkSkills*™ series uses the same format. This uniform structure enables you to gradually master each skill.

Build on What You Know

This section introduces the skills by making connections to your daily life or in the workplace. The Essential Skills that you will be learning are clearly identified on the first page of the lesson. The "In Real Life" features connect and apply these skills to workplace scenarios.

Develop Your Skills

This section provides in-depth instruction on the skills or strategies that are the focus of the lesson. Examples illustrate how to apply skills and strategies in workplace situations, and questions guide you through the steps you will use to successfully apply these strategies on your own. The "Got It?" feature summarizes the key points you should remember from each lesson.

Apply Your Knowledge

Practice the skills and strategies you have learned. A "To Do List" gives you a reminder of key points and processes, while another "In Real Life" scenario provides an opportunity to take what you have learned and apply it to another workplace scenario. "Think About It!" gives you a chance to reflect on what you have learned and the different ways that you can use it in the workplace.

Test Your WRC Skills

Each lesson concludes with a *Test Your WRC Skills* section. These pages use questions modeled after those you will see on the National Work Readiness Credential assessment to give you practice applying the skills you have learned. Answers are provided at the back of the book.

Assessments

The *WorkSkills*™ series includes a number of tools to help you assess what you already know, identify the skill areas on which you may need to focus, and monitor your progress as you study. As you have seen, the lessons include a number of opportunities for you to use what you know and what you are learning in real-world applications of important workplace skills. In addition, there are several other opportunities, both within the books and online, for you to practice applying your skills by answering questions that are similar to those you will see on the National Work Readiness Credential assessment.

Online Pretests

Before you begin your studies in this book, take the Online Pretest, which is a full-length practice version of the National Work Readiness Credential assessment. The questions on the Pretest mimic those on the National Work Readiness Credential assessment in style, format, and content.

Chapter Assessments

Student Book Chapter Assessments

At the end of each chapter in the book, questions similar to those on the National Work Readiness Credential assessment allow you to determine whether you have mastered the Essential Skills that you learned in the chapter.

Additional Online Chapter Assessments

The Online Chapter Assessments allow you to evaluate your mastery of the skills taught in the chapter you have just completed, as well as skills taught in previous chapters of the book. The questions are similar in style to those you will see on the National Work Readiness Credential assessment.

Online OFFICIAL Work Readiness Practice Tests

The Online OFFICIAL Work Readiness Practice Tests are the full-length practice version of the National Work Readiness Credential assessment and are endorsed by the National Work Readiness Council. Use your results to assess what you have learned and where additional study may be needed.

Answers and Explanations

You can quickly check your answers for each student book Chapter Assessment question, as well as the *Test Your WRC Skills* sections, in the *Answers and Explanations* section in the back of the book. This feature provides the correct answer, as well as a full explanation for why each answer choice is correct or incorrect. When taking the Online Chapter Assessments, you will get automated feedback.

The National Work Readiness Credential

Today's adult education and workforce development programs face significant challenges in adequately preparing adults for entry into the workplace. However, the National Work Readiness Council has issued a new credential based on the *Equipped for the Future* standards. According to the NWRC, the new National Work Readiness Credential assessment assists educational professionals in:

> **"**Getting and keeping a job is an important first step to meeting the demands of adulthood and self-sufficiency.**"**
>
> —Joe Mizereck,
> Acting Executive Director of the
> National Work Readiness Council

- Assessing a learner's skills and needs.

- Creating learning experiences based on a simple standard of integrated skills and tasks.

- Providing competency goals that are useful for instruction and aspirational for learners.

- Aligning instruction to a standard defined by business.

- Demonstrating performance outcomes to funding organizations.

The National Work Readiness Credential assessment is designed to assess a worker's on-the-job skills in four areas: reading, math, situational judgment, and active listening.

Steck-Vaughn's *WorkSkills*™ Series

If adult education and workforce development programs are to prepare students to pass the National Work Readiness Credential assessment, they need material that assists them in making the connection between what they learn in the classroom and how they can use that information in the workplace. Steck-Vaughn's *WorkSkills*™ series is designed to prepare adult learners to successfully pass the National Work Readiness Credential assessment and earn the National Work Readiness Credential. The series has been designed to cover all Domains and Essential Tasks, as identified by the National Work Readiness Council. Mastery of these tasks is viewed as necessary for adults to effectively be prepared for entry-level positions.

Steck-Vaughn's *WorkSkills*™ is endorsed by the

Benefits That Set *WorkSkills*™ Apart

- Contextualized and integrated instruction
- Focus on real-world, workplace contexts and skills
- Gradual-release model of modeling-practice-application-test
- Written for non-traditional learners: approachable tone and accessible format
- Controlled readability, ranging from 7.0–7.9
- Print, online, and audio components
- Assessments that mimic the actual National Work Readiness Credential assessment:
  - Online Pretests
  - Online OFFICIAL Work Readiness Practice Tests
  - Chapter Assessments (available in print and online)
  - *Test Your WRC Skills* sections
- Answer keys with explanations/solutions
- Workplace Glossary

Components of the *WorkSkills*™ series include:

Available in Print

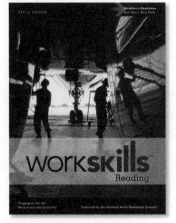

WorkSkills™ Reading

WorkSkills™ Math

WorkSkills™ Situational Judgment and Active Listening

Available Online

- Online Pretests
- Downloadable Scenarios/Audio Scripts for Active Listening
- Additional Chapter Assessment questions
- Online OFFICIAL Work Readiness Practice Tests
- Online Teacher Lessons, available as printable PDFs

For online assessments and instructor support, visit www.mysteckvaughn.com/WORK.

Steck-Vaughn's *WorkSkills*™ Situational Judgment and Active Listening

All three books in the *WorkSkills*™ series have been designed to address the Work Readiness Domains and Essential Tasks. The *WorkSkills*™ Situational Judgment and Active Listening book integrates these two key areas into five chapters that address all of the Situational Judgment and Active Listening Domains and Essential Tasks.

I. Solve Problems and Make Decisions

II. Active Listening

III. Resolve Conflict

IV. Cooperate with Others

V. Take Responsibility for Learning

Soft Skills for the Workplace

Of course, strong reading and math skills are essential for entry-level workers to succeed in today's workplace. Of critical importance as well are the broad range of "soft skills," including:

- Setting Goals
- Working as Part of a Team
- Resolving Conflict
- Making Decisions
- Cooperating with Others
- Personal Skills

- Negotiating
- Taking Initiative
- Communicating Effectively
- Solving Problems
- Listening Actively
- Interpersonal Skills

The sole focus of *WorkSkills*™ Situational Judgment and Active Listening is teaching effective strategies to help students develop their own soft skills. Ample practice and application opportunities are provided, all in the context of realistic workplace scenarios. An integral part of the *WorkSkills*™ series, this contextualized instruction enables students to transfer new skills from book to workplace.

Workforce Readiness
Real World. Real Skills.

An Integrated Approach

WorkSkills™ Situational Judgment and Active Listening has been designed with an integrated approach to teaching situational judgment and active listening skills. The book instructs students on the soft skills necessary to respond to situational judgment scenarios and questions, and then gradually integrates strategies for active listening into the lessons. The integration works as follows:

- Chapter 1 introduces students to effective decision-making and problem-solving strategies.
- Chapter 2 focuses on the teaching and application of active listening skills.
- Chapters 3–5 integrate active listening skills into each situational judgment lesson.

Scenarios for Situational Judgment

Following instruction on skills and strategies, the lessons include numerous scenarios that require students to apply on-the-spot situational judgment, such as conflict resolution or negotiating skills, to real-world work situations. Students must consider what they have learned, and then respond to questions about the scenario by deciding the *best* action that an individual should take. In addition, they must also decide on what would be the *worst* action to take.

Strategies for Active Listening

Many students are not auditory learners and can benefit from instruction on strategies for listening actively. The Active Listening lessons in this book teach students strategies for becoming effective listeners, such as how to identify the important aspects of a conversation. Students actively listen to online audio scenarios, drawn from real-world workplace situations. Then students respond to questions that require them to respond to the audio scenario. For these active listening questions, students choose the one best response.

 For classrooms where online services are not available to students, the active listening scenarios are scripted and provided in the online teacher resources. This allows teachers to print the scripts and read them aloud to students.

Purchase the
National Work Readiness Credential assessment

Steck-Vaughn has proudly partnered with the National Work Readiness Council to be the exclusive distributor of the National Work Readiness Credential assessment. Contact your sales representative for more details. You may also contact our customer service team at **800-289-4490** or visit our website at **www.steckvaughn.com/adulted**.

The *WorkSkills*™ Situational Judgment and Active Listening Lessons at a Glance

These pages explain the setup of the Situational Judgment and Active Listening lessons. This allows you to see the differences and similarities.

Situational Judgment

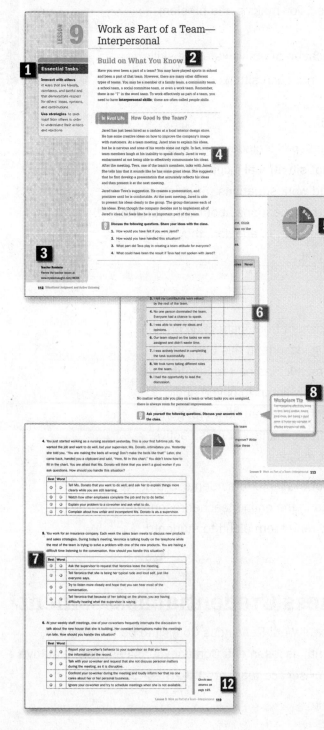

1 **Essential Tasks**
Lessons focus on critical Essential Tasks.

2 **Controlled Readability**
The readability of instruction is controlled, averaging between 7.0–7.9.

3 **Online Teacher Lessons**
The online teacher lessons, available as printable PDFs, provide instructors with strategies and activities to help students master the skills.

4 **Situational Judgment Realistic Workplace Scenarios**
Students are presented with realistic workplace scenarios that require problem solving, conflict resolution, and decision making.

5 **Four-Step Process**
The gradual-release model of instruction enables learners to Build, Develop, and Apply new skills. Then learners Test their skills to assess their understanding.

6 **Situational Judgment Graphics-Based Material**
Students practice interpreting and completing graphics-based information, such as charts, tables, and signs.

7 **Situational Judgment Best and Worst Answer Choices**
The Situational Judgment *Test Your WRC Skills* and Chapter Assessment items mimic the National Work Readiness Credential assessment, requiring students to choose the best and worst response to each scenario.

Active Listening

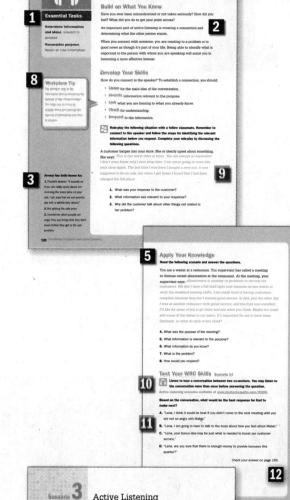

8 Workplace Tip

These examples and helpful tips enable students to apply what they learn in the lesson to the workplace.

9 Active Listening

Realistic Workplace Scenarios

Students are presented with realistic listening scenarios that help them develop and apply active listening strategies.

10 Active Listening

Scenarios/Audio Scripts

Students listen to realistic workplace audio selections, which they hear on their computer or as read aloud by their instructor.

11 Active Listening

One Best Answer Choice

The Active Listening *Test Your WRC Skills* and Chapter Assessment items mimic the National Work Readiness Credential assessment, requiring students to choose the one best response to each question.

12 Answers and Explanations

For each *Test Your WRC Skills* and Chapter Assessment question, students can quickly check their answers and also review a full explanation for each possible choice.

1 Solve Problems and Make Decisions

Solving problems and making decisions in the workplace require critical observation of the situations you encounter. In this chapter, you will learn how to effectively solve problems using a five-step process and interpret signs in the workplace using critical thinking.

Problem Solving: The First Steps

Essential Tasks

Identify problem to be solved or decision to be made

Understand and communicate root causes of problem

Generate possible solutions that address the root causes of the problem

Build on What You Know

On a daily basis, you may encounter problems at home, at school, or at work. When problems arise, they may seem like a hassle. However, many problems present great opportunities to change things and make them better. In the workplace, every type of job has responsibilities that may present various problems. These problems often involve one or more of the following:

- equipment and machinery
- schedules and deadlines
- disagreements between people
- customer service complaints

Your job as an employee is to identify and solve problems that arise in different situations. Some problems may be minor and take just a few minutes to solve. Others may be more complex, and solving them may require a great deal of time and careful consideration.

In this lesson, you will learn and practice strategies to help you identify, communicate, and solve problems in the workplace.

In Real Life Access Denied

After two years of hard work, Jamaal was promoted and given a new workspace. In his new cubicle, he has a new phone and a new computer. Yesterday Jamaal set up his voicemail and computer. Today he arrived at work and tried to log on to his computer, but he received this message: "Invalid Password: Access Denied." He retyped his username and re-entered his password several times, but he kept receiving the same error message.

With a classmate, discuss the following questions. Share your ideas with the class.

1. What is Jamaal's problem?

2. Can Jamaal solve this problem on his own? Why or why not?

3. How would you handle the problem?

Teacher Reminder
Review the teacher lesson at
www.mysteckvaughn.com/WORK

18 Situational Judgment and Active Listening

The 5-Step Problem-Solving Process

Problems in high-pressure workplace situations can cause you stress. However, you will feel less stressed out and more in control if you are equipped with the necessary tools to solve these problems. Using the five-step process to develop effective **problem-solving skills** will help prepare you to deal with problems in the workplace:

1. **Identify the problem.** What is the problem to be solved or the decision to be made?

2. **Gather information about the situation.** What information do I need in order to understand the problem and its causes?

3. **List possible solutions that address the problem.** What are some ways to solve this problem?

4. **Evaluate the possible results of each solution.** What will be the result of each solution? What are the pros and cons?

5. **Decide on the best solution.** Which solution will have the best results?

The first three steps of the problem-solving process will help you examine and define your problem. These **problem analysis** steps are essential for understanding the problem you are facing. The last two steps of the process are about choosing the best solution to the problem. You can use these two steps when you understand the problem completely and are ready to make a decision.

> **Workplace Tip**
> Effective problem-solving skills:
> - Help you reduce stress.
> - Prepare you for difficult situations.

Think about problems you have faced at home or at work and complete the following chart. Then discuss the questions below.

	Often	Sometimes	Never
I feel calm when facing problems at work.			
I feel stressed when facing workplace problems.			
I find it easy to identify problems.			
I gather information before trying to solve a problem.			
I consider more than one solution before trying to solve a problem.			
I find it easy to decide on the best solution to a problem.			

4. When facing a problem, what are your strengths?

5. Which problem-solving skills would you like to improve?

6. Why are problem-solving skills important in the workplace?

Develop Your Skills

Remember, the first three steps of the problem-solving process involve analyzing and understanding the problem, and the last two are about deciding on the best solution. This lesson focuses on the problem analysis steps of the process. Using these steps to better understand a problem will set you up for success when it's time to decide on a solution.

Identify the Problem

It may seem obvious, but before you can determine how to solve a problem, you must recognize what it is. Try to remain calm and focus on the exact problem you are facing. Avoid getting upset or frustrated, since that will only make solving the problem more difficult. Then restate the problem in your own words. Focus on using a calm, rational approach to help you establish a solid foundation for the entire problem-solving process.

Discuss the following scenario with a classmate. Then answer the questions that follow.

You work at a cable company. An angry customer calls and complains that she is being charged for a premium cable plan instead of the basic cable plan that she requested. This is the third time she has received a bill with the same error, and she wants to cancel her cable service.

1. What is the customer's problem?

2. What are the first steps you should take to solve the problem?

Workplace Tip

When you gather information about a problem, remember to:

- Focus on relevant facts.
- Don't waste time trying to assign blame.

Gather Information

After you identify what the problem is, the next step toward finding a solution is to look for the **root causes** of the problem. Identifying root causes requires good detective work. You will need to gather information to help you determine what caused the problem. When you get to the root of the problem, you may discover that the cause of the problem is not what you initially thought.

When gathering information, be sure to focus on information that is **relevant**. This step may sound easy, but sometimes people focus on information that doesn't really matter. If you waste time with irrelevant information, such as who is to blame, the problem will remain unsolved and may get worse. To stay focused on relevant information, ask yourself these questions:

Who has the problem?	**Where** did it happen?
What is the problem?	**Why** did the problem happen?
When did it happen?	**How** can the problem be solved?

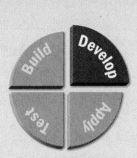

 Read the scenario and discuss the questions that follow.

Mia works at an animal shelter. Her favorite part of the job is helping pets find happy homes. When she is not helping pets get adopted, Mia feeds the animals and cleans their cages. Every afternoon, Mia rinses out each dog's kennel using the large water hose near the kennel entrance. One afternoon, Mia goes to wash out the kennels, and the hose is gone.

   3. What is Mia's problem?

   4. What steps might Mia take to identify the root cause of the problem?

   5. What information in the scenario is not relevant to solving the problem?

List Possible Solutions

Once you have identified the problem and gathered relevant information, you are ready to list possible solutions that address the problem. This step of the problem-solving process involves **brainstorming**, or generating ideas. Depending on the problem, you can list possible solutions on your own, or you may collaborate with co-workers. To guide your brainstorming, ask yourself questions, such as: *Have I had a problem like this in the past? What did I do then?*

Eventually you will weigh your options and assess their pros and cons, but brainstorming is most effective when you keep an open mind and list as many solutions as you can think of without making any hasty judgments. You may need to modify solutions later when you assess your list.

 Read the scenario. Then brainstorm at least three possible solutions with a classmate.

Tran asked for two days off work, and her supervisor approved them. She then submitted an E-Request online. When she received her work schedule the following week, she was surprised to see that she was scheduled to work on the days she had requested off. After talking to other employees, Tran discovered that the online E-Request system was not processing all requests properly.

   6. What are some possible solutions to this problem?

> **GOT IT?** **Identifying and analyzing problems will help you resolve workplace issues. To analyze a problem:**
>
> - Identify the exact problem you are facing.
>
> - Gather relevant information to find the root causes of the problem.
>
> - Brainstorm a list of possible solutions that address the root causes.

Answer Key

1. The customer has an error on her bill.

2. Remain calm, focus on the problem, and restate what the problem is.

3. Mia's problem is that the hose is gone.

4. Answers will vary, but Mia might look for the hose and ask co-workers if somebody borrowed the hose and forgot to return it.

5. Possible answer: The details about Mia's favorite part of her job are not relevant to solving the problem.

6. Answers will vary, but Tran may begin by talking to her supervisor.

To-Do List

Remember to follow these steps when applying your knowledge:

- ❏ **Identify the problem**
- ❏ **Gather relevant information**
- ❏ **Brainstorm ways to solve the problem**

Apply Your Knowledge

Solving problems in the workplace requires you to identify the problem, understand its root causes, and generate possible solutions.

As you read the following scenarios, think about the different types of problem-solving skills you have learned in this lesson. Select what you think is the best response and the worst response to each situation.

1. You work as a data entry clerk for a law firm. At the beginning of your shift, a lawyer gives you an important twenty-page assignment to complete. You work hard all day to complete this assignment, and you save your work frequently. At the end of your shift, you are entering the last page of data when your computer crashes. You restart your computer, and the document you were working on is not in your folder. What should you do?

   A. Shut down your computer and leave for the day.

   B. Tell the lawyer you need more time to complete the assignment.

   C. Start the assignment over and create a new document.

   D. Call your supervisor to explain what happened and ask for help.

Best Answer		Worst Answer	

2. Ella is a nurse's aide in the emergency room at a hospital. After working night shifts for a year, Ella meets with the head nurse in her ward and requests to switch to day shifts. The head nurse says that the hospital is short-staffed, and he needs Ella to work night shifts because there are no other aides to cover the shifts. What should Ella do?

   A. Apply for a job in a different ward of the hospital.

   B. File a written complaint about the head nurse.

   C. Ask aides working day shifts if they will switch shifts with her.

   D. Continue working night shifts for another year.

Best Answer		Worst Answer	

3. Your boss hands you a sales report and asks you to make ten copies and bring them to this morning's meeting. Two copies come out of the machine, and then the copier starts beeping and showing this flashing message: "ERROR: Paper Jam in Tray 1." What should you do?

   A. Go to a copier on another floor to make your copies.

   B. Open Tray 1 and carefully remove the jammed paper.

   C. Create a sign that says "Out of Order" and tape it to the copier.

   D. Leave and bring your boss the two copies of the sales report.

Best Answer	

Worst Answer	

In Real Life Put Your Skills to Work!

You are a security guard at a shopping mall. In the past month there have been shoplifting incidents in three of the stores at the mall. Your supervisor calls an emergency meeting to discuss this problem. At the meeting, your supervisor asks you and your co-workers to gather information about these incidents and to come up with some ideas for reducing theft at the mall.

Think about the problem you are facing and put your skills to work! What kinds of questions would help you gather relevant information about the problem? Brainstorm a list of questions and possible solutions.

Workplace Tip

When making your list, did you think about:

- Defining the problem?
- Finding the root causes of the problem?
- Possible solutions that address each root cause?

Answer Key

1. The best answer is D. Asking for help will help you identify and solve the problem. The worst answer is A. Shutting down your computer and leaving for the day does nothing to identify or solve the problem.

2. The best answer is C. Looking for an aide to switch shifts addresses the root cause of the problem. The worst answer is B. Filing a written complaint about the head nurse is not justified and will not solve the problem.

3. The best answer is B. Removing the paper from Tray 1 is the fastest and most responsible way to resolve the situation. The worst answer is D. Leaving the machine with a paper jam does not solve the problem, and bringing your boss two copies of the report does not complete your task.

Think About It!

How can analyzing a problem help you solve it?

How will you apply problem analysis to problems you encounter on the job?

Your ability to identify and analyze problems can help you succeed in all types of workplace environments and situations. Following the first three steps of the problem-solving process will help you understand a problem completely and identify possible solutions. Understanding the problems you encounter in the workplace may also help you prevent future workplace problems and disagreements.

Test Your WRC Skills

Select the best response and the worst response to each situation.

1. You are a waiter at a restaurant. One night the restaurant is very busy, and a customer stops you on your way to the kitchen. The customer tells you that there are no more paper towels in the restroom. How should you handle this situation?

Best	Worst	
○	○	Calmly explain that the restrooms are not your problem.
○	○	Apologize to the customer and tell another waiter to take care of it.
○	○	Apologize and tell the customer you will take care of it right away.
○	○	Ask your manager to install hand dryers in the restrooms.

2. You just started working at a day care center. You notice that some of the toys in the toddlers' activity areas are broken. Some of the toys have broken pieces with sharp edges. How should you handle this situation?

Best	Worst	
○	○	Ask a co-worker to throw away the broken toys.
○	○	Remove the broken toys and ask how you should dispose of them.
○	○	Tell your supervisor that the toys need to be fixed immediately.
○	○	Tell the toddlers that they should not use the broken toys.

3. In a staff meeting, your manager announces that she will be conducting performance reviews over the next two weeks. She says that she will post a sign-up sheet outside of her office with each employee's name and available time slots for the reviews. She asks each employee to sign up for a one-hour time slot. You walk by her office the next day and see the sign-up sheet, but your name is not on the list. How should you handle this situation?

Best	Worst	
○	○	Wait a week and bring up the issue in the next staff meeting.
○	○	Explain the error to your manager and ask her to add your name.
○	○	Do nothing and hope that your manager will correct the mistake.
○	○	Ask your co-workers why they think your name is not on the list.

4. You work for a carpet cleaning company. Your cleaning team is scheduled to clean the carpets of a large office building. As you are loading equipment into the company van, you accidentally break the wheel off of one of the shampooer machines. How should you handle this situation?

Best	Worst	
○	○	Tell your supervisor that another employee broke the wheel.
○	○	Admit what you did and ask your co-worker to fix the wheel.
○	○	Complain to your co-workers about the quality of the machine.
○	○	Explain the accident to your supervisor and ask how to proceed.

5. You work at an auto repair shop. A customer wants to buy a tire and explains which type he wants. When you check your inventory, you discover that your shop doesn't have that type of tire in stock. You explain to the customer that the tire is out of stock, but that you can order it for him. The customer gets angry and complains that your store never has the parts he needs for his car, and he always has to wait while the parts are on special order. How should you handle this situation?

Best	Worst	
○	○	Apologize for the inconvenience and offer the customer an approved discount for special orders.
○	○	Explain to the customer that you do not make the ordering decisions and give him a coupon for a free oil change.
○	○	Apologize to the customer and explain that the person who manages the shop's inventory has been on vacation.
○	○	Tell the customer that if he is unhappy with your shop, he should take his business elsewhere.

6. The factory where you work implemented a new policy that requires all employees in your work area to wear safety goggles. This morning the safety manager informed all employees that there are boxes of safety goggles in the factory's three supply rooms. Before your shift begins, you go to one of the supply rooms to get goggles. You search all the shelves and find that there are no safety goggles left. How should you handle this situation?

Best	Worst	
○	○	Complain to the safety manager that there are no safety goggles.
○	○	Don't wear eye protection, and be extra careful in your work area.
○	○	Ask to borrow a co-worker's safety goggles.
○	○	Check the other supply rooms for safety goggles.

Check your answers on page 158.

Problem Solving: Look for Solutions

Essential Tasks

Evaluate options and select the one most likely to succeed based on apparent causal connection and appropriateness to the context

Plan and implement chosen solution

Monitor effectiveness toward a solution

Build on What You Know

Have you ever thought about something you've done and wished you had handled it differently? Perhaps you realized too late that you could have accomplished your task more quickly or cheaply. Maybe you could have avoided the frustration or confusion that resulted from your choices. Poor decisions often leave us asking, "Why did I do that?"

People make decisions every day, both in their personal lives and at work. Sometimes the decisions are fairly easy to make. You might choose what to eat for lunch or what shirt to wear to work. However, **decision making** can also be very challenging. It is not always easy, for example, to decide the best way to get a promotion or how to calm an angry customer. This lesson will teach you strategies for making some of those tough decisions in the workplace.

In Real Life   May I Make a Suggestion?

Sahar is the assistant manager at a coffee shop. The owner, Mr. Ricci, believes that receiving customer feedback will help him improve his business. He places a suggestion box by the door and encourages customers to fill out cards with comments, concerns, and suggestions.

Mr. Ricci asks Sahar to read the cards and determine the best solutions for any problems or complaints. Sahar finds that many customers are frustrated with the long morning lines. The suggested solutions, however, vary a great deal. Several customers recommend adding another register. Others believe it would be more efficient to have some workers take orders, while others make the coffee. One customer demands that loyal customers who come in daily be allowed to go to the front of the line. Another suggests a self-serve option for people who just want a simple cup of coffee or tea.

 Discuss the following questions with the class.

1. Are the suggested solutions useful? Why or why not?

2. What might some consequences be to each solution?

3. Based on the possible solutions, what decision would you make? Why?

Teacher Reminder
Review the teacher lesson at
www.mysteckvaughn.com/WORK

Making Decisions to Solve Problems

In Lesson 1, you learned about the five-step problem-solving process:

1. **Identify the problem.**

2. **Gather information about the situation.**

3. **List possible solutions that address the problem.**

4. **Evaluate the possible results of each solution.**

5. **Decide on the best solution.**

Lesson 1 focused on the first three steps, which are about analyzing and understanding the problem. In this lesson, you will focus on the last two steps, which focus on decision making. Decision making means evaluating the possible solutions to a problem and then choosing the best one.

How Do You Make Decisions?

Being aware of how you naturally tend to make decisions can help you understand your decision-making strengths and weaknesses. It can also help you understand how the people you work with might approach decision making.

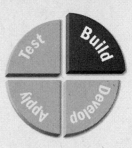

Read about each decision-making style. Then answer the questions.

Practical	Instinctive
Practical decision makers are realistic. Their aim is to reach a solution quickly and efficiently. They are very focused on the end goal, and they tend to base their decisions on facts rather than emotions.	Instinctive decision makers usually let their emotions guide them. They might make decisions quickly without thinking about all the consequences. In addition, they may change their decisions as they learn more about a problem.
Cooperative	**Examining**
Cooperative decision makers like to ask others what they think before making a decision. They want to make sure that a decision is made with others' feelings in mind. They prefer to work as a team in order to solve problems.	Examining decision makers take a great deal of time to understand every possible option. They thoroughly research solutions and consequences. They compare solutions against each other and may look for creative alternatives.

> **Workplace Tip**
>
> Use these decision-making styles as general guidelines to understand how you and others make decisions. Knowing how other people make decisions can help you relate to them in the workplace.

4. What is your decision-making style? Do you use different styles in different situations?

5. What are some possible strengths of each decision-making style? What are some weaknesses?

6. What might it be like to work with someone who has a different style than yours?

Develop Your Skills

No matter what your decision-making style is, when you make a decision your ultimate goal is to choose the best solution from the available options. Practice the steps below to help you make the right choice.

Evaluate and Decide on the Best Solution

For problems that do not have a single obvious answer, you must decide on the **best solution** from several options. Usually the best solution is a solution in which everybody "wins." This means everybody gets something they want or need. In the real world, it is difficult to find a solution in which *everybody* gets *everything* they want. Decision making usually requires you to evaluate which solution will get the best results for the most people.

When you evaluate the possible solutions to a problem, think about the **pros and cons** of each option. Pros are the reasons for something, and cons are the reasons against it. T-charts are useful for listing the pros and cons of each solution. Ask yourself these questions when thinking about pros and cons: *Who "wins"? Who "loses"? Can I do this? Does this solution solve the problem?*

> **Workplace Tip**
>
> When considering who "wins" or "loses" in a possible solution, it may be helpful to get input from the people or groups involved. They may give you more information to help you make your decision.

Read the following scenario and T-charts. Then answer the questions.

Several customers have complained that the packages they received do not contain the products they ordered. You find that the problem is caused by the shipping department employees' failure to identify products correctly. You come up with four possible solutions to the problem. Then you make the following T-charts to evaluate each one.

Option 1: Replace all employees in the shipping department.

Pros	Cons
• New employees might do a better job. • Somewhat likely to solve the problem.	• The company will have to hire and train many new employees. This takes a lot of time and money. • Current employees will lose their jobs. • Not realistic.

Option 2: Give current shipping department employees more training.

Pros	Cons
• Current employees already have knowledge of how things work, so training won't take as long. • Current employees will be better trained. • Current employees will keep their jobs. • Very likely to solve the problem. • Realistic.	• Extra training will cost the company time and money.

Option 3: Do all the packaging yourself to be sure it is done correctly.

Pros	Cons
• Customers would get the correct products. • Likely to solve the problem.	• Not realistic because it is too much work for one person. • Current employees would have nothing to do. • Company would lose money because fewer shipments would go out on time.

Option 4: Apologize to customers and explain the problem.

Pros	Cons
• Realistic.	• Customers will not get the correct orders. • Current employees will continue to make the same mistakes. • Will not solve the problem.

1. Which options solve the problem? Which are realistic?

2. How can these charts help you evaluate your options?

3. Which solution gets the best results for the most people?

Plan, Apply, and Check

Once you decide on the best solution, make a plan of action. Think about what steps you need to take to make your solution work, and then follow these steps.

As you apply your solution to the problem, check to see how well it is working. Ask yourself: *Is the solution solving the problem? What changes, if any, need to be made?* You will only face more problems if you do not solve the original problem. It's worth your time to make sure your solution works!

Read the following scenario. Discuss with a classmate why the solution doesn't work and what could be changed.

Tanisha goes out for lunch every day, which causes her to be late to her afternoon meetings. She decides that she will need to skip lunch in order to be on time. During the next meeting, Tanisha's stomach begins growling very loudly, and she can't concentrate.

GOT IT? **The last steps in the problem-solving process are about making good decisions. Remember to:**

• Evaluate possible solutions by listing pros and cons.

• Select the solution that gets the best results for the most people.

• Make a plan, carry out the plan, and check that the solution works.

To-Do List

Remember to follow these steps when applying your knowledge:

- ❏ **Evaluate possible solutions**
- ❏ **Select the best solution**
- ❏ **Plan, apply, and check the solution**

Apply Your Knowledge

You can use the problem-solving process to solve situational judgment problems in the workplace.

As you read the following scenarios, use the decision-making skills you have learned to select the best response and the worst response to each situation.

1. You deliver flowers for a local florist. On your way to make a delivery, you encounter very heavy traffic. There has been an accident, and cars are backed up for miles. You are fairly new to the city and worry that you will get lost if you try to take another route. There is no way you will be able to drop off the flowers by noon, as the customer requested. What should you do?

   A. Patiently wait in traffic and deliver the flowers as soon as you can.

   B. Call the customer from your cell phone to explain the situation and inform her that the delivery will be late.

   C. Give up on trying to make the delivery and drive back to the shop.

   D. Wait for your supervisor or the customer to call and ask you why the flowers have not yet been delivered.

Best Answer		Worst Answer	

2. You are getting ready for your first day of work at a local sandwich shop. You are not sure what to wear, but you remember from your interview that the employees dress casually. You decide to wear a t-shirt, jeans, and flip-flops. When you arrive, the manager tells you that all employees must wear closed-toed shoes. You are embarrassed because you did not know about this policy. What should you do?

   A. Explain that you didn't know the policy and offer to go change your shoes since you live just a few blocks away.

   B. Tell the manager that you can wear what you want because the policy is not posted for employees to see.

   C. Check to see that other employees are wearing closed-toed shoes, and then ask if anyone has an extra pair.

   D. Apologize to the manager and tell him you will try to remember to wear closed-toed shoes next time.

Best Answer		Worst Answer	

Put Your Skills to Work!

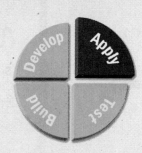

The furniture warehouse where you work has just received a shipment of small glass tables. You are responsible for unloading the tables and moving them to the other end of the building. As you take one of the tables from the truck, it slips from your hands and breaks. You look around and find that nobody saw the table break. Though accidents happen in the warehouse, you don't want your supervisor to think you are a careless worker.

Think about the problem you are facing and put your skills to work! What options do you have to solve your problem? How will you evaluate each possible solution? How will you identify the best solution?

Workplace Tip

When making your decision, did you think about:

- The pros and cons of each solution?
- Selecting a solution that gets the best results for the most people?
- Making a plan and checking to make sure it will solve the problem?

Think About It!

What kinds of decisions do you think you will need to make in your workplace?

What can you do to improve your decision-making skills?

Some decisions you make at work will be important and affect a lot of people. Others will be small and affect only you. Though many decisions will be quick and easy to make, you may sometimes find yourself spending a long time researching options and consequences. You can improve your decision-making skills by carefully evaluating all possible solutions to a problem. Many poor decisions result from not thinking about consequences. If you evaluate the possible solutions, choose the best one, and stick to a plan to make sure your solution works, you won't have to think back on your choice and say, "I wish I had done that differently!"

Answer Key

1. The best answer is B. Letting the customer know what is going on and assuring her that the delivery will be made as soon as possible is the best course of action. The worst answer is C. It is your supervisor's job, not yours, to decide if the delivery needs to be canceled. Only make decisions that are in your power to make.

2. The best answer is A. It is important to explain to your manager why you made your initial decision, and then try to correct the situation. The worst answer is B. It is the manager's role to know and enforce policies. Do not assume that because you are initially unaware of a policy that you do not have to follow it.

Test Your WRC Skills

Select the best response and the worst response to each situation.

1. You are working at an outdoor construction site. Weather forecasters have predicted a severe cold front will come through your area today. Sure enough, temperatures begin to drop rapidly in the afternoon. You know that the client has been putting pressure on your supervisor to make up time from other delays. How should you handle this situation?

Best	Worst	
○	○	Continue working despite the potential danger because it is important to keep the client happy.
○	○	Check with your supervisor to see if it is safe to work, and trust that he will keep you and the client informed of the situation.
○	○	Seek shelter from the cold and hope that the weather will clear up shortly, since weather forecasters are often wrong.
○	○	Tell your supervisor that it is too cold to work and you need to go home right away.

2. You recently received an evaluation of your work as a customer service representative. Your supervisor suggested that you work on speaking more clearly to customers. You decide to take a public speaking workshop to improve your communication skills. What is the next step in this situation?

Best	Worst	
○	○	Practice speaking to a friend.
○	○	Find out if the workshop is helping.
○	○	Complete the workshop.
○	○	Find a workshop to take.

3. As a product promoter for a new sports drink, it is your job to give out samples at sporting events. People at recent events have been taking multiple samples, causing your supply to run out early. You decide that in the future you will implement a one-sample-per-person policy. At your next event, a man approaches your table and starts to pick up three samples. How should you handle this situation?

Best	Worst	
○	○	Keep quiet and assume that he is taking the extra samples to his friends.
○	○	Tell the customer that he is being selfish and doesn't need three samples.
○	○	Let him take the extra samples and tell the next person about the policy.
○	○	Explain your policy and ask that he take only one sample.

4. You work as an assistant manager at a toy store. Several employees express to you that they are not able to work enough hours because other employees sign up for more shifts than they should. You decide that you need to make a schedule to balance employee work hours. When you post the schedule, an employee is surprised to see that some of her hours have been cut, and she asks for them back. How should you handle this situation?

Best	Worst	
○	○	Tell the employee you will consider her request when you make the next schedule.
○	○	Explain why you made the schedule and offer the employee the option of filling in for employees who need to miss a shift.
○	○	Ask the manager for advice and hope that she can make the schedule more acceptable to the employees.
○	○	Give the employee more hours by taking away another employee's hours.

5. You have been working as a postal service clerk for three months. You do not like being inside all day, so you decide you would rather be a mail carrier. You take the mail carrier test and do very well. Now you plan to continue working as a clerk until a mail carrier position becomes available at the post office where you work. What is the next step in this situation?

Best	Worst	
○	○	Check job postings for a mail carrier position.
○	○	Apply for a mail carrier position.
○	○	Begin work as a mail carrier.
○	○	Accept a position as a mail carrier.

6. You work as a cashier at a large supermarket. It is a busy time of day, and there are five customers in your checkout line. As you are ringing up the first customer, the receipt printer runs out of paper. You look around your counter for an extra paper roll, but there isn't one. How should you handle this situation?

Best	Worst	
○	○	Ask the customer if she wants a receipt and hope that the answer is no.
○	○	Close your register and direct the customers to other checkout lines.
○	○	Explain that you need to refill the printer, and quickly get a spare paper roll from another counter.
○	○	Write out receipts by hand until an available manager can get you another paper roll.

Check your answers on page 159.

Skills for the Workplace

Signs in the Workplace

Signs in the workplace have many purposes. They may give information, such as warnings and cautions, or instructions in case of an emergency. You can think of signs as short, important messages in the form of pictures and words. The illustrations and text on a sign are designed to give you the information you need quickly and efficiently.

Thinking about the signs you see in the workplace will help you do your best at work—and may help keep you safe. When you see a sign in the workplace, ask yourself these questions:

- **What is the message?** What do the pictures show? What do the words say?

- **What is the purpose?** Why is the sign there? Does it share information about directions, health and safety, or how to do something? What should people do after reading it?

- **Who is the intended audience?** Who needs this information? Thinking about the message and the purpose of the sign can help you determine the audience.

Workplace Scenario

The management of a new restaurant placed this sign in the bathroom:

Employees must wash hands for at least 20 seconds before returning to work.

1. What is the message of this sign? *Employees must wash their hands for at least 20 seconds before returning to work.*

2. What is the purpose of this sign? Why is it important? *The sign tells all employees to wash their hands so the food stays safe and customers do not get sick.*

3. If you were a cook at the restaurant, would you need to follow these instructions? What if you were a customer dining at the restaurant? *Yes, a cook is a restaurant employee and would need to follow the instructions on the sign. The sign is intended for employees only, not customers.*

Workplace Practice

You work in a medical facility. You have brought your lunch to work and need to put it in a refrigerator until your lunch break. You see a refrigerator in a nearby room with this sign posted on it.

1. What does the sign mean?

2. Should you put your lunch in the refrigerator? Why or why not?

The biohazard sign indicates that the refrigerator contains materials that are dangerous to humans. You should not put your lunch in the refrigerator because your food could become contaminated.

It's Your Turn!

1. You work at a cleaning company and see the sign below. What is the message of this sign?

2. You are working at a construction site, and you see a sign that shows a hard hat and the words "Hard hat must be worn at all times." What is the purpose of this sign? Who is the intended audience?

3. You are making copies when the copier stops working and begins flashing an error code. You check for jammed paper, but there is none. You see this sign on the copier. How should you handle this situation?

For copier repairs, call: 555-555-1000.

Workplace Tip

If someone posts a sign in your workplace, the information on it is probably important for employees to know. If you do not understand a sign in your workplace, ask!

It's Your Turn! Answer Key

1. Mixing bleach with glass cleaner can be deadly.

2. The purpose is to prevent injuries. The audience is construction workers and visitors to the construction site.

3. You should call the number on the sign and report the problem.

Chapter 1 Assessment

Select the best response and the worst response to each situation.

1. You work at a day care. A parent of one of the children tells you she is unhappy because the snacks provided by the day care contain too much sugar. How should you handle this situation?

Best	Worst	
○	○	Tell the parent you understand her concern and that you'll speak with your supervisor about the snacks.
○	○	Offer special snacks just for the concerned parent's child.
○	○	Tell the parent you'll look into providing snacks with less sugar, but then don't do anything.
○	○	Instruct the parent to bring snacks with less sugar for her child.

2. Several co-workers at the landscaping company where you work have been complaining of small injuries. You notice that some of them have not been wearing the appropriate goggles and gloves. How should you handle this situation?

Best	Worst	
○	○	Tell the owner of the landscaping company that your co-workers refuse to wear goggles and gloves.
○	○	Remind your co-workers that wearing goggles and gloves will help them avoid getting injured.
○	○	Buy your co-workers new safety goggles and gloves.
○	○	Don't do anything because it is not your problem.

3. A client keeps complaining that she is not receiving her packages on time. You have determined that the mail clerk at your company has not been sending the packages in a timely manner. How should you handle this situation?

Best	Worst	
○	○	Send the packages yourself to make sure they arrive on time.
○	○	Assure the client that the packages were sent on time even though you know they weren't.
○	○	Talk to the clerk about the problem and ask if he needs help getting the mail out on time.
○	○	Immediately tell your supervisor about the client's complaint.

4. You work as a file clerk at a medical office. As you are working, you suddenly realize that you incorrectly filed a large batch of patient records because you labeled the folders incorrectly. How should you handle this situation?

Best	Worst	
○	○	Tell the doctors in the office that some patient records were misfiled.
○	○	Don't do anything and hope no one notices your mistake.
○	○	Ask another co-worker to file the records correctly for you.
○	○	Immediately tell your supervisor and offer to correct your mistake.

5. You think your company should implement a recycling program. You are bothered that paper, cans, and bottles pile up in the company's garbage cans, only to end up in landfills. When you explain your concerns to your supervisor, he says he doesn't think a recycling program is a priority, but you can do something about the issue if it bothers you. How should you handle this situation?

Best	Worst	
○	○	Collect all the recyclable items yourself and take them to a recycling center after work.
○	○	Let the issue go since your supervisor doesn't think it is a priority.
○	○	Tell your supervisor that his attitude is environmentally irresponsible.
○	○	Talk to the office manager about possible ways to implement a recycling program in the office.

6. The company where you work has this sign near the elevator. Your company is having a fire drill, and you see a co-worker trying to use the elevator. How should you handle this situation?

Best	Worst	
○	○	Get on the elevator with your co-worker because there is no actual fire.
○	○	Tell your co-worker that nobody else is using the elevator.
○	○	Point to the sign and explain why the elevator shouldn't be used.
○	○	Report your co-worker's behavior to your supervisor.

7. Your company has an open position in the communications department. The position requires basic knowledge of Web design. You do not know any Web design but would like to be considered for future positions in the communications department. What would be a good next step in this situation?

Best	Worst	
○	○	Try to learn Web design by looking at the design of various Web sites.
○	○	Enroll in a Web design course at your local community college.
○	○	Learn Web design during work hours using a company computer.
○	○	Ask a co-worker to teach you Web design during breaks.

8. You work as a cook in a school cafeteria. For the past month, one of the other cooks has been leaving food out to spoil. You decide that the next time the cook makes this mistake, you will speak with her about how to fix the problem. The following week, you find food that has been left out. How should you handle this situation?

Best	Worst	
○	○	Kindly explain to your co-worker why it is important to not let food spoil.
○	○	Talk about your co-worker's mistake to others and see what they think.
○	○	Let your co-worker keep messing up so she gets fired.
○	○	Take over your co-worker's tasks to make sure they get done correctly.

9. The hospital where you work has this sign hanging outside an operating room. A co-worker is having a loud conversation on his cell phone outside of the operating room. How should you handle this situation?

Best	Worst	
○	○	Tell your supervisor that the hospital needs to post a bigger sign outside of the operating room.
○	○	Politely interrupt your co-worker and explain why people need to be quiet near the operating room.
○	○	Don't do anything—you don't want to interrupt his phone call.
○	○	Tell your co-worker to stop being so loud on the phone.

10. The restaurant where you work has this sign hanging in the restroom. You overhear a co-worker saying that he doesn't wash his hands every time he uses the restroom because it takes too long. How should you handle this situation?

Best	Worst	
○	○	Immediately tell your manager to fire your co-worker for disobeying the hand-washing policy.
○	○	Tell your co-worker he should wash his hands because the sign says he should.
○	○	From now on, ask your co-worker if he washed his hands every time he comes back from the restroom.
○	○	Explain the reasons why all employees should wash their hands after using the restroom.

11. You work as a recruiter for a community college. You have noticed that when you and your manager travel to high schools to recruit students, your manager always forgets to bring important materials. This has caused problems because you often cannot provide students with all the information they need. How should you handle this situation?

Best	Worst	
○	○	Spend your breaks gathering all the needed materials before each trip.
○	○	Ask your co-workers what they would do in this situation.
○	○	Don't do anything—it's your manager's problem, not yours.
○	○	Offer to help gather the materials before traveling to high schools.

12. You work as a city bus driver. Lately, you have not been sleeping well, and you are often tired on the job. How should you handle this situation?

Best	Worst	
○	○	Ignore how tired you are and keep driving your scheduled routes.
○	○	Talk to your supervisor to discuss taking time off to see a doctor.
○	○	Tell your supervisor you want to quit your job because you are too tired.
○	○	Get other drivers to cover your shift when you are tired.

For more Chapter 1 assessment questions, please visit www.mysteckvaughn.com/WORK

Check your answers on page 160.

2 Active Listening

When you listen actively, you use various strategies to help you understand what a speaker is saying and why. In this chapter, you will learn why active listening is important. You will also learn how to become a better listener by recognizing how people speak and use body language to communicate.

Purpose for Active Listening

Build on What You Know

Has anyone ever said to you, "Are you really listening to me?" or "Didn't you hear a word that I just said?" Think about it. You're listening to someone, and suddenly you're thinking about something else—maybe errands you have to run after work or what you want for dinner. Most people find themselves in this situation occasionally. Fortunately, there are steps you can take to help you become a more focused, active listener.

Actively listening to and understanding what someone says is an essential and highly valued skill in the workplace. Listening is a process that involves three elements: the listener, the speaker, and the message itself. **Active listening** requires the listener to focus on what another person is saying and how he or she says it in order to understand the message.

In this lesson, you will learn reasons why active listening is important in the workplace, in both formal and informal situations. You will also learn skills that will help you become a better active listener.

In Real Life | An Important Exception

Sandra works for a catering company. She is responsible for taking catering orders and helping distribute work among food preparers and cooks. A customer calls her and says: *I would like to order forty of your daily special for an important luncheon I am hosting this Thursday at 12:00 P.M. One of the meeting attendees is allergic to nuts. I need to know whether your special includes anything made with nuts. If so, I'll need to make a substitution for that person's dish.*

Discuss the following questions. Share your ideas with the class.

1. What is this customer's purpose for calling?

2. What details must Sandra understand to perform her job?

3. What important information about the order should Sandra make sure to pass on to the food preparers and cooks?

4. What might happen if Sandra didn't listen to or understand everything the customer said?

Teacher Reminder
Review the teacher lesson at
www.mysteckvaughn.com/WORK

Consider the Purpose

Your purpose for listening or speaking is the *reason* you listen or speak. The reason differs depending on the situation and what role you are in. As a speaker, your job is to share information clearly so that a listener can understand you. As a listener, your job is to focus on the information a speaker is sharing. When you interact with co-workers, how well you listen affects how well you are able to do your job. It also affects how well you build relationships in the workplace.

Consider the Setting

In an **informal setting**, such as a one-on-one conversation with a co-worker, people often speak and behave in a friendly, casual, and relaxed way. In a **formal setting**, such as a staff meeting or a meeting with a supervisor, people normally speak and behave in a professional manner. In both settings, however, it is important to keep in mind your purpose for listening.

Active Listening Tips

When you practice active listening, you not only hear the words another person is saying, but you also make an effort to understand his or her message completely. Use these tips to help you become a better active listener.

- **Pay Attention** Put aside distracting thoughts and listen carefully. If you are interacting in person, pay attention to the speaker's gestures and body language. Also notice the speaker's tone of voice.

- **Show You Are Listening** You can use gestures, expressions, and body language to show you understand what someone is saying. You might also use short **verbal cues**, such as "yes" and "uh–huh."

- **Respond Appropriately** Show respect by allowing the speaker to finish before you respond. Then you can respond by asking questions, voicing concerns, or acknowledging that you have understood what the speaker has said.

Listen to the Scenario Scenario 1

Listen to hear a conversation between an employee and his supervisor. Then discuss the following questions.

Active Listening Scenarios are available at **www.mysteckvaughn.com/WORK**.

5. How can you tell that Susan is Ben's supervisor?

6. Why did Susan call Ben in to meet with her?

7. Based on this conversation, what should Ben do?

Workplace Tip

Remember to block out any distractions and focus on the speaker to fully understand his or her message.

Develop Your Skills

Active listening in the workplace requires that you pay close attention to what a speaker says and how he or she says it. Use the following skills to help you become a better active listener.

Practice the Active Listening Tips

When you interact with a co-worker, remember to put aside distractions and pay attention. Use body language, gestures, and facial expressions to show you are listening and interested in what your co-worker says. Finally, remember to allow the speaker to finish speaking before responding. Following these tips will help you better understand the message your co-worker is trying to share.

Role-play the following excerpt from Scenario 1 with another student. Then answer the questions and discuss your ideas with the class.

Susan: How are you doing? How was your weekend?

Ben: My weekend was very busy, but I'm doing well. How was yours?

Susan: I had a great weekend, thanks. Though it sounds like mine was a little more relaxing than yours. In fact, that's what I hoped to meet with you about. Do you mind shutting the door and having a seat?

1. If you overheard this part of the conversation, would you describe it as mainly formal or informal? Explain your answer.

2. How does Susan's last line change the tone of the conversation?

Workplace Tip

Remember the difference between a formal and an informal setting. Pay attention to the way speakers behave and interact to determine whether the setting is formal or informal.

The 5 Ws and H

When you read actively, you focus on the most important details. The same is true when you listen actively. To focus on the most important details, ask yourself the questions below:

- **Who** is speaking?
- **What** is the person saying?
- **When** is the conversation taking place?
- **Where** is it occurring?
- **Why** is the person telling you this?
- **How** is the person speaking and behaving?

Answering these questions will help you understand a speaker's full message.

Practice with the 5 Ws and H

Asking yourself the 5 W and H questions will help you listen actively when someone is speaking. The answers will help you determine how to respond in both formal and informal situations.

 Role-play the following excerpt from Scenario 1 with another student. Then fill out the 5 Ws and H chart and discuss the questions.

Susan: In fact, that's what I hoped to meet with you about. Do you mind shutting the door and having a seat? Ben, our company has certain policies in place for a reason. Take, for example, our overtime policy. The overtime policy is in place for your good and for the good of the company.

Ben: Sorry about that, Susan. I would have checked in about working with the weekend crew at the site, but it slipped my mind. I'm really committed to making sure this building job is done right and on time.

Susan: I understand that. However, in the future it's important that you notify me or another supervisor about overtime work you wish to sign on for. Not only do we need to monitor your hours to make sure we're not overworking you, but we need to make sure you are compensated fairly for all the hours you work.

3.	Who?	
4.	What?	
5.	When?	
6.	Where?	
7.	Why?	
8.	How?	

9. Would you describe this part of the conversation as formal or informal? Explain your answer.

10. Why has Ben been taking on extra work at the site?

11. What is Ben's purpose for listening to Susan?

GOT IT?   **Effective listening starts with you! When you interact with a co-worker, remember to:**

- Pay attention and clear your mind of any distractions.

- Show you are listening by using gestures and short verbal cues.

- Allow a speaker to voice his or her thoughts and then respond in a way that is appropriate to the situation.

Answer Key

1. Informal. The tone is friendly and casual.

2. The tone becomes more serious and professional.

3. Susan and Ben

4. Susan is explaining why the company has an overtime policy; Ben apologizes.

5. A day early in the workweek

6. In Susan's office

7. Susan is meeting with Ben because he violated the overtime policy.

8. Susan and Ben speak and behave professionally.

9. Formal. Both Ben and Susan speak and behave in a professional manner.

10. He is committed to making sure the job is done right and on time.

11. To learn a policy that will affect him at his job

To-Do List

Remember to follow these steps when applying your knowledge:

❑ **Listen carefully**

❑ **Answer the 5 Ws and H**

❑ **Think about how you would respond**

Apply Your Knowledge

Being an effective listener requires that you apply different types of skills when you interact with co-workers.

As you read the following scenarios, think about tips and skills you have learned. Select the best response for each question.

1. Ben has just finished working a weekend overtime shift at a building site. Because he has been working extra hours on the weekend, he sometimes takes a long lunch break to take care of personal errands. After his shift, Susan, his supervisor, calls him over to discuss a problem. She says: *Ben, I really appreciate your willingness to work overtime on the weekend. But today you took a two-hour lunch break. I noticed you deducted the time from your overall hours for the day, and I know you have personal errands you need to take care of. However, company policy states that lunch breaks should not exceed one hour. This policy is in place to make sure all employees are present during the same hours so that jobs are completed on schedule. In the future, please restrict your lunch breaks to one hour.*

   Based on this conversation, what should Ben do?

   A. He should stop signing up for overtime shifts on the weekend.

   B. He should make sure his lunch breaks last no more than one hour.

   C. He should ask a co-worker to help with his personal errands.

   D. He should ask permission before he takes a long lunch break.

2. How should Ben respond to his supervisor?

3. Susan has a meeting with fellow supervisors to discuss the budget and deadline on a current building project. When she arrives at the meeting a few minutes early, a co-worker named Jon says: *These meetings are a complete waste of time. We'd be better off skipping the meetings and getting back to work at the job site. We need to stop spending time talking about our budget and start picking up the pace on this job . . .*

   Susan disagrees, but Jon is still talking. What should Susan do?

   A. Allow Jon to finish speaking before responding with her point of view.

   B. Interrupt Jon because she disagrees with his opinion about the meeting.

   C. Allow Jon to finish and then ask him to behave more professionally.

   D. Keep her ideas to herself until the very end of the meeting.

Practice with the Scenario Scenario 1

Listen to hear a conversation between an employee and his supervisor. You may listen to the conversation more than once before answering the question.

Active Listening Scenarios are available at www.mysteckvaughn.com/WORK.

4. Based on what Susan told Ben, which of the following statements is true?

   A. Ben can work as much overtime as he wants, as long as he asks permission afterward.

   B. Ben is no longer authorized to work overtime.

   C. Ben may work overtime hours, but first he must get approval from Susan or another supervisor.

   D. The more overtime Ben works, the more valuable he is to the company.

In Real Life Put Your Skills to Work!

Have a conversation with a classmate. Ask the student to tell you about his or her workplace, family, or something which he or she enjoys doing. When you have finished your conversation, present what you learned about your classmate to the rest of the class.

 Think about the problem you are facing and put your skills to work! How did active listening help you gather the information for your presentation? How was your informal conversation different from your formal presentation?

> ### Workplace Tip
> When listening to your classmate, did you:
> • Pay close attention?
> • Show you were listening?
> • Respond appropriately?
> • Ask yourself the 5 W and H questions?

Think About It!

What active listening skills do you need to practice most to help you succeed in your workplace?

How can you practice these skills outside of work?

Listening actively will help you in the workplace, but you can practice these skills at any time. Remember to use the tips you've learned to help you focus on the speaker's message and respond appropriately to the situation. You can also use the 5 W and H questions to monitor your understanding.

Answer Key

1. B

2. Possible answer: Ben should acknowledge that he understands and will follow the policy in the future.

3. A

4. C

Test Your WRC Skills

Use Active Listening Scenarios 1 and 2 to respond to the following questions. You may listen to scenarios more than once before answering the questions.

Active Listening Scenarios are available at www.mysteckvaughn.com/WORK.

Please listen to Scenario 1 to hear a conversation between an employee and his supervisor.

1. Based on this conversation, what should Ben do if he would like to keep his job in good standing?

A.	○	Make a better impression with Susan and the other managers.
B.	○	Work more overtime to make sure the building job is done on schedule.
C.	○	Ask for approval before working any more overtime hours.
D.	○	Relax more on the weekend so he is more productive during the week.

Please listen to Scenario 1 to hear a conversation between an employee and his supervisor.

2. Why is Susan **MOST** likely worried about Ben working too much overtime?

A.	○	She wants to make sure Ben enjoys his time off on the weekends.
B.	○	Ben is not as strong of a worker when he's worked too many hours.
C.	○	She wants to make sure Ben doesn't work more hours than other employees.
D.	○	Ben forgot to report his overtime, which caused a payroll error.

Please listen to Scenario 1 to hear a conversation between an employee and his supervisor.

3. Based on this conversation, why does the company have policies in place?

A.	○	To make sure building jobs are completed on schedule
B.	○	To keep employees from working too many hours
C.	○	To encourage employees to take on extra responsibilities
D.	○	To help the company and the employees succeed

Please listen to Scenario 1 to hear a conversation between an employee and his supervisor.

4. What is expected of Ben in his future with the company?

A.	○	He will follow company policies.
B.	○	He will complete all of his work on time.
C.	○	He will stop working overtime.
D.	○	He will memorize all company policies.

Please listen to Scenario 2 to hear an orientation speech for new employees.

5. What is the purpose of this speech?

A.	○	To congratulate employees and remind them to ask for help
B.	○	To welcome new employees and describe their responsibilities
C.	○	To quiz employees on the names of dental instruments and machines
D.	○	To read through a few important company policies

Please listen to Scenario 2 to hear an orientation speech for new employees.

6. Based on the speech, what should employees do to learn more about their responsibilities?

A.	○	Ask the trainer for assistance.
B.	○	Read the company policies.
C.	○	Set up an appointment with the dentist.
D.	○	Read the orientation documents.

Please listen to Scenario 2 to hear an orientation speech for new employees.

7. According to the speech, why do new employees need to start by learning basic skills?

A.	○	So they can help keep the office running smoothly
B.	○	To prepare them to become dentists
C.	○	So they can assist other employees during training
D.	○	To help them better understand their orientation documents

Please listen to Scenario 2 to hear an orientation speech for new employees.

8. Based on the speech, which of the following statements is **TRUE**?

A.	○	Employees who are not comfortable and confident when assisting the dentist will need to repeat the training program.
B.	○	All of the duties the dental assistants are expected to perform will be easy for them to learn.
C.	○	Some of the dental assistants' duties will be difficult to learn, but help will be available.
D.	○	Most of the new employees who begin the program will not make it all the way through on-the-job training.

Check your answers on page 161.

Strategies for Active Listening

Essential Tasks

Identify typical words and phrases found in simple oral communication (e.g., interpersonal, telephone)

Make notes to support comprehension and memory

Request change in pace and/or word usage from speaker

Identify where message confirms or contradicts previous knowledge

Build on What You Know

Have you ever walked away from a conversation with a co-worker and felt unsure about details from the conversation or what action you should take next? Both in formal and informal situations, it is sometimes hard to focus attentively on a speaker and fully process what he or she has said. A speaker may be difficult to understand or may share too much information for you to easily remember. Fortunately, there are active listening strategies you can practice to help you better understand a speaker's message.

You've already learned that recognizing the purpose and the setting of the conversation can help you listen actively and respond appropriately. In this lesson, you will learn several active listening strategies to help you become a more effective listener. Active listening will help you learn, follow directions, and succeed in the workplace.

In Real Life   Keeping Pace

Jorge works as a bus driver. Part of his job is making sure he completes his route on schedule. His supervisor has gathered Jorge and the other bus drivers for a brief meeting. He says: *Due to the marathon this weekend, our routes will change slightly on Saturday. You will make the same stops you normally do, but you will need to take detours in order to avoid road closures and complete your routes on time. Please pick up a revised route map at the front office and see me if you have any questions. Your stop schedule is unchanged, so make sure to pay close attention to time and your progress during your shift.*

 Discuss the following questions. Share your ideas with the class.

1. Based on the meeting, what should Jorge do?

2. How should Jorge respond if a passenger asks whether the marathon will cause delays in the bus schedule?

3. What might happen if Jorge didn't listen to or understand everything his supervisor said?

Teacher Reminder

Review the teacher lesson at www.mysteckvaughn.com/WORK

Use Active Listening Strategies

Active listening requires focus and attention to detail. In Lesson 3, you learned to use the 5 W and H questions to help you listen actively and focus on the most important details. When you listen, remember to ask yourself the following questions:

- **Who** is speaking?
- **What** is the person saying?
- **When** is the conversation taking place?
- **Where** is it occurring?
- **Why** is the person telling you this?
- **How** is the person speaking and behaving?

The 5 W and H questions will help you understand the big ideas in a speaker's message. But sometimes understanding the big ideas is not enough. You may need to understand specific information or directions; or you may need to remember several important details and use them later. When this is the case, the following strategies can help:

- **Recognize Clue Words** Listen for typical words and phrases people use in various situations. These words can provide you with the clues you need to understand how the ideas in the speaker's message are related.

- **Ask for Help** Know that it is appropriate to ask the speaker to slow down or explain a term that was used. The speaker wants you to understand. Otherwise, he or she would not be speaking to you!

- **Summarize What You Hear** Repeating to the speaker the main ideas or details in the message will help you remember it. It will also give the speaker the chance to correct anything you may not have understood completely.

- **Make Notes** Jot down a few short notes when presented with a lot of information or with tasks you must remember to complete. Your notes will help you remember the information you need to get the job done.

Listen to the Scenario Scenario 3

Listen to hear a conversation between an employee and her supervisor. Then discuss the following questions.

Active Listening Scenarios are available at **www.mysteckvaughn.com/WORK**.

4. Why is Jack concerned about Kati's work performance?

5. Why is Kati having problems at work?

6. Based on the conversation, what should Kati do?

Workplace Tip

Don't make a bad situation worse. If you have problems meeting a deadline at work, let your supervisor know ahead of time. It is the responsible thing to do, and your supervisor may be able to help with the problem.

Develop Your Skills

When you practice active listening, you block out distractions and pay attention not only to what a speaker says, but also to how it is said. Use the following strategies to help you become a more effective listener.

Recognize Clue Words

Some words and phrases are so common that we hardly even notice them. We hear phrases like "Please hold," "No problem," and "Do you have a minute?" all the time without realizing that they give clues about the conversation. Other **clue words** show how the ideas in a speaker's message are related. Consider the words in the chart below.

Clue Words	These words indicate:
first, next, then, last	the order of ideas or steps
because, as a result, consequently	causes and effects
such as, for example	that one or more examples will follow
also, in addition to	that two or more ideas are related
both, like, similar	comparisons, or how things are alike
however, but, although	differences or an alternate idea
mainly, primarily, above all	the most important factor or idea
luckily, unfortunately	how the speaker feels about the idea

Ask for a Change

Have you ever listened to someone who talks very fast or too softly for you to hear? At times, you may need to ask someone to slow down or repeat something. Asking someone to rephrase, or use different words, can also help you understand terms or ideas that may be unfamiliar.

 Read this excerpt from Scenario 3 aloud to another student. Read Jack's dialogue too quickly, and then too quietly. Talk about how this changed your partner's ability to understand. Then discuss the questions.

Jack: Let me finish, Kati. It is not just about being late for work. You've also missed two major deadlines in the last few weeks. As a result, we are behind schedule and running out of time on the VPN presentation. What's going on? What can I do to help you get back on track?

1. Which clue words does Jack use to show how his ideas are related?

2. If Kati could not hear Jack or understand something he said, what should she do?

Summarize and Make Notes

Sometimes you can use all of the active listening strategies you have learned so far and still not quite understand the speaker's message. You may be confused because the message does not make sense or because it conflicts with other information you already know. In these situations, it is helpful to **summarize** by repeating a speaker's main ideas in your own words. When you summarize the speaker's message, you give yourself another chance to understand it. You also give the speaker a chance to correct any misunderstandings.

At other times, you might understand everything that is said but need help remembering the most important information. Making notes will help in this kind of situation. When you are listening and it becomes clear that there is a lot of important information you will need to remember later, write down a few notes to help you remember the main points. Place a check box next to any items that list tasks you need to complete. The notes will help you remember the information you need, and you can check off the items as you complete each task.

👥 **Role-play this excerpt from Scenario 3 with another student. Then answer the following questions and discuss your thoughts with the class.**

Kati: Jack, I'm really sorry about being late and missing deadlines. There has just been so much going on at home that I let a few things slip here at work. It'll get better. I just need a little more time to work things out.

Jack: I hear you, Kati, and I wish I could give you more time, but we just don't have it. We've got a week to get back on track and finish that presentation. After that, you can take some time off if you need it. Kati, you have been an excellent employee in the past, and I know you can be again. Let's work together and make sure that happens.

3. What could Kati do to make sure she understands Jack's message?

4. What might happen if Kati does not understand what she needs to do?

5. What notes could Kati make to help her improve her job performance?

GOT IT? | **Making sure you understand what you hear in the workplace is up to you. When you are listening:**

- Focus on the speaker and listen for clue words.

- Ask the speaker to speak up, slow down, or rephrase when needed.

- Summarize by repeating the main points in your own words.

- Make notes about information you need to remember or use later.

Answer Key

1. *Also, as a result*

2. She should ask him to repeat or clarify the information.

3. She could repeat the main ideas in her own words.

4. If Kati does not understand that she needs to improve her job performance, she might lose her job.

5. Possible answer: Be on time; presentation due in one week

To-Do List

Remember to follow these steps when applying your knowledge:

❑ **Listen for clue words**

❑ **Ask for a change**

❑ **Summarize**

❑ **Make notes**

Apply Your Knowledge

Being an effective listener requires that you apply different types of strategies when you interact with co-workers.

As you read the following scenarios, think about the listening strategies you have learned. Select the best response for each question.

1. Kati went back to work after her meeting with Jack and began to work on her part of the presentation. She quickly discovered that she needed more information about the software program she was supposed to use. Kati's co-worker, Lucinda, has worked on many presentations in the past and knows the software very well. Kati would like to ask her for some pointers. However, Lucinda is from another country, and Kati sometimes has trouble understanding her. What should Kati do to make sure that she gets the information she needs?

   A. Interrupt Lucinda when she starts talking too fast.

   B. Worry about it later, since she can always go back and ask her again.

   C. Make a list of questions and send them to Lucinda via e-mail.

   D. Ask Lucinda for clarification when she does not understand something.

2. That afternoon, Jack attended a meeting about an upcoming change in the company-provided insurance plans. He took notes to make sure he had all the information he needed. At one point, the insurance representative said the following: *All employees' current coverage will remain in place for another two months. During that time, the Human Resources department will distribute and process the enrollment forms for the new insurance plans. It is important that all employees have their forms completed and turned in by July 1 so that the forms can be processed in time for the change.*

   Which of the following would Jack be most likely to write in his notes?

   A. Enrollment forms due July 1

   B. Human Resources department

   C. New insurance plans

   D. Current coverage in place

3. In what other circumstances might you find it helpful to take notes in the workplace?

Practice with the Scenario Scenario 3

Listen to hear a conversation between an employee and her supervisor. You may listen to the conversation more than once before answering the question.

Active Listening Scenarios are available at **www.mysteckvaughn.com/WORK**.

4. In the conversation, Jack says, "Let me finish, Kati." Why does he do this?

   A. He's the boss, so he can do what he wants.

   B. He wants to provide further clarification about his concerns.

   C. He doesn't want to hear what Kati has to say.

   D. He needs to finish the conversation to attend a meeting.

In Real Life   Put Your Skills to Work!

The company you work for is having a supervisors' meeting to discuss important new policies and an upcoming project. Your supervisor will be out of town on the day of the meeting, and she has asked you to attend on her behalf. She would like you to tell her about the new policies and project when she returns from vacation.

Think about the problem you are facing and put your skills to work! What kinds of information will you need to gather for your supervisor? What strategies can help you understand and remember the new policies and project?

> **Workplace Tip**
>
> When preparing to listen to the meeting, did you think about:
> - Using the 5 Ws and H?
> - Listening for clue words?
> - Asking for a change of pace or word use when needed?
> - Summarizing the information in your own words?
> - Making notes about the most important information?

Think About It!

What active listening strategies are most valuable to you in your workplace?

How do the strategies help you?

There are several strategies you can use to help you be an effective listener in the workplace. You may find some of the strategies you've learned more useful than others for your particular job. Each strategy, however, can be used in and out of the workplace to help you focus on and better understand what a speaker says.

Answer Key

1. D

2. A

3. Answers will vary.

4. B

Test Your WRC Skills

Use Active Listening Scenarios 3 and 4 to respond to the following questions. You may listen to the scenarios more than once before answering the questions.

Active Listening Scenarios are available at **www.mysteckvaughn.com/WORK**.

Please listen to Scenario 3 to hear a meeting between an employee and her supervisor.

1. If Kati took notes during the meeting, which of these comments would **MOST** likely be written?

A.	○	Report back to Jack in a few weeks
B.	○	One week to finish presentation
C.	○	Write to kids' school about late arrival
D.	○	Excellent employee in the past

Please listen to Scenario 3 to hear a meeting between an employee and her supervisor.

2. How should Kati respond if she did not understand the phrase "back on track"?

A.	○	She should ask, "Can you please explain what you mean by 'back on track'?"
B.	○	She should ask someone else what the phrase means after the meeting.
C.	○	She should say, "I have no idea what you are talking about."
D.	○	She should ignore the phrase and listen to everything else Jack has to say.

Please listen to Scenario 3 to hear a meeting between an employee and her supervisor.

3. Based on Jack's advice, what should Kati do?

A.	○	Take a leave of absence so she can work out her personal problems.
B.	○	Write an apologetic letter to other employees working on the presentation.
C.	○	Stop letting things slip at work and go back to being an excellent employee.
D.	○	Ask Jack how he gets his kids off to school and still shows up to work on time.

Please listen to Scenario 3 to hear a meeting between an employee and her supervisor.

4. How does Kati confirm that she understands Jack's message and what action is necessary?

A.	○	She says, "No problem, I am always here to help."
B.	○	She says, "Jack, I'm really sorry about being late and missing deadlines."
C.	○	She says, "I just need a little more time to work things out."
D.	○	She says, "I won't let you or the company down."

Please listen to Scenario 4 to hear an informative recording from a career center.

5. Based on the message, Smart Start is a service available to which of the following job seekers?

A.	○	Workers who have recently lost a job
B.	○	Single parents
C.	○	First-time job seekers
D.	○	Currently employed individuals

Please listen to Scenario 4 to hear an informative recording from a career center.

6. If you are a first-time job seeker, which of the following notes would you **MOST** likely write?

A.	○	Wide range of services
B.	○	Smart Start, prep for interview
C.	○	Single Parent Connection
D.	○	Layoffs, job match

Please listen to Scenario 4 to hear an informative recording from a career center.

7. Which of the following would be the **BEST** course of action if you needed additional information now and were unable to wait for a client representative?

A.	○	Call back another time.
B.	○	Contact someone who has used the career center before.
C.	○	Visit the career center.
D.	○	Access the career center's Web site.

Please listen to Scenario 4 to hear an informative recording from a career center.

8. Which of the following services would be of **MOST** interest to a single parent with young children?

A.	○	Childcare services
B.	○	Assistance with job applications
C.	○	Connecting with other job seekers
D.	○	Assistance with writing résumés

Check your answers on page 162.

Skills for the Workplace

Body Language

Understanding body language will help you become a better listener and communicator at work. **Nonverbal cues,** such as facial expressions and physical gestures, give clues about what someone is feeling or thinking. Tone of voice can give more information about what a person is saying as well as how he or she feels about it.

Some body language is clearly inappropriate for the workplace. For example, rude gestures are unprofessional and reflect poorly on the person making them. Other nonverbal cues are more subtle. For example, standing too close to someone as you talk may be interpreted as intimidating or invasive. Speaking too softly or not making eye contact might make people think you are shy or lack confidence.

Below are some other common nonverbal cues that you may encounter. Notice that some of them have more than one possible meaning.

Body Language	Meaning
tilted head	curiosity, sympathy
looking down at the floor	shyness, evasiveness
crossed arms	defensiveness
touching one's face, fidgeting	nervousness
rolling eyes	disrespect

Workplace Scenario

While Linda was telling her boss about her weekend plans, she noticed that her boss made very little eye contact and kept looking at her watch. Her boss also glanced at her computer screen every few seconds.

1. What body language did Linda's boss use? *She made very little eye contact, looked at her watch, and glanced at her computer screen.*

2. Given the context, what do you think these nonverbal cues were saying? *Linda's boss was not interested or did not have time to listen to her.*

3. How should Linda respond to her boss's nonverbal cues? *She should cut her story short or offer to share her plans at another time.*

> **Workplace Tip**
>
> An interested listener maintains eye contact and demonstrates his or her understanding with facial expressions and nods. Use these strategies when you are listening, and keep them in mind when you are speaking, too.

Workplace Practice

Your co-worker Sanjay just gave a short presentation to the sales department. During his presentation, Sanjay looked down at the floor and fidgeted with his pen. He also spoke so quietly it was difficult to hear him.

1. What body language and tone of voice did Sanjay use?

2. What message did his body language and tone of voice convey?

3. What should Sanjay do to improve his presentation skills?

Sanjay looked down at the floor, fidgeted with his pen, and spoke too quietly. This conveyed that he was nervous, shy, and lacked confidence. To improve his presentation skills, Sanjay should try to make more eye contact with his audience, avoid fidgeting, and speak in a louder voice.

It's Your Turn!

1. Your department is having a meeting about low sales figures. You look over and notice your supervisor shaking his head. Every once in a while, he lets out a loud sigh. Toward the end of the meeting, he pounds his fist on the table and says in a loud voice, "We need to reconsider our strategy!"

   A. What do these actions tell you about how your supervisor is feeling?

   B. Would this be a good time to meet with your supervisor to discuss a promotion? Why or why not?

2. Your co-worker has a deadline for a project this afternoon. You stop by to ask how things are going, and he glances up at you and quickly looks at the floor. He mutters "fine" under his breath and then turns back to his work.

   A. What does your co-worker's reaction tell you?

   B. What could you do to improve this situation?

3. You work in a medical office. A new doctor has joined the team, and you want to make her feel welcome. What nonverbal cues can you use to help you accomplish your goal?

4. You and a co-worker are operating a large piece of machinery in a factory, and you notice that his shirt is untucked. This is dangerous because your co-worker could become injured if his shirt gets stuck in the machinery. The factory floor is very loud, so you need to rely on nonverbal cues to get your co-worker's attention and tell him about the problem. How could you convey your message?

It's Your Turn! **Answer Key**

1A. He is conveying frustration and possibly anger.

1B. No. Your supervisor clearly is upset, which makes this the wrong time to bring up a promotion.

2A. His body language tells you that things actually are not fine. If things were going well, your co-worker would not have looked away and probably would have given you a clearer response.

2B. You could ask your co-worker if there is anything you can do to help with the project.

3. Possible answer: You should make eye contact and smile when you welcome her.

4. Possible answer: Wave to get his attention, use facial expressions to indicate a problem, and pantomime tucking in your shirt to indicate what the problem is.

Chapter 2 Assessment

Select the answer you think best responds to the question.

1. A computer technician at your company is explaining how to reset the password for your e-mail account. Why should you take notes while the technician speaks?

   A. Because it is polite to take notes when a co-worker speaks to you

   B. So you can do the technician's job when he is out sick or on vacation

   C. Because it is important to practice your note-taking skills whenever possible

   D. So you have instructions available in case you need to reset your password in the future

2. You are finishing work on a bid for a large printing project. The client calls to ask for the "estimated time of arrival" of the bid. How should you respond?

   A. Ask the client if your company should still submit a bid.

   B. Explain how long the printing project should take to complete.

   C. Tell the client when you think you can send him the completed bid.

   D. Tell the client you will send the bid in an hour, even though you can't.

3. Your supervisor gathers everyone to discuss the problem of excessive tardiness. You know that you sometimes arrive at work a few minutes late. After listening to your supervisor, what should you do to keep your job in good standing?

   A. From now on, try to leave your house ten minutes earlier each morning.

   B. Come to work on time, but leave 15 minutes earlier in the evening.

   C. Keep coming to work at the same time, and hope your supervisor doesn't notice.

   D. Tell your supervisor when other employees arrive at the office late.

4. At the energy company where you work, your department manager tells you that all customer complaints should now be routed to the resolution department. On your first day of training, you had learned that complaints should be routed to your direct supervisor. How should you handle this situation?

   A. Complain to your supervisor about the new directions.

   B. Start sending complaints to the resolution department.

   C. Keep sending complaints to your direct supervisor.

   D. Tell the department manager she doesn't know what she's talking about.

Scenario 5

Listen to hear an announcement about a food safety training session. You may listen to the announcement more than once before answering the questions.

Active Listening Scenarios are available at www.mysteckvaughn.com/WORK.

5. What is expected of an employee who has attended a safety and sanitation training session in the past?

   A. The employee must attend this session, since new procedures have been introduced.

   B. The employee must come to work on Friday at 9:30 A.M., even if he or she is not scheduled to work.

   C. The employee should attend the session to set a good example for newer employees.

   D. The employee should attend the session again if he or she wants to review safety and sanitation practices.

6. Who is **MOST** likely the speaker of the segment about the training session?

   A. Kitchen manager

   B. Cook

   C. Waiter

   D. Dishwasher

7. If an employee did not understand the word *pathogens*, how should he or she respond?

   A. "What are you talking about?"

   B. "Why would we want to prevent pathogens?"

   C. "Could you please tell me what *pathogens* are?"

   D. "I don't understand the point of this training session."

Check your answers on page 163.

 For more Chapter 2 assessment questions, please visit www.mysteckvaughn.com/WORK

CHAPTER

3 Resolve Conflict

Handling conflict effectively in the workplace is an important skill that involves a number of steps. In this chapter, you will learn how to recognize and acknowledge conflict, resolve conflict, and overcome barriers to good communication.

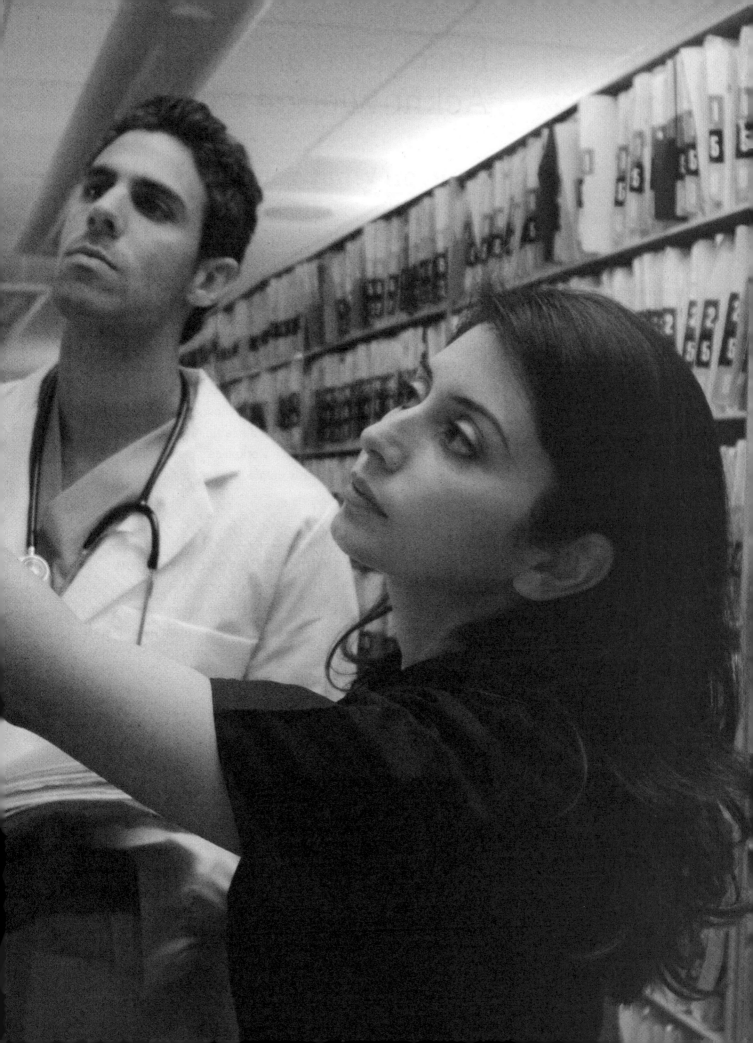

Recognize and Acknowledge Conflict

Essential Tasks

Acknowledge conflict by defining conflict

Acknowledge conflict by identifying areas of agreement and disagreement

Acknowledge conflict by accurately restating conflict with some detail and examples

Build on What You Know

Have you ever had trouble making weekend plans with a friend? Maybe you wanted to go to a movie, but your friend wanted to go to a concert. What did you do when this happened? Did you go along with your friend's idea, your idea, or something totally different?

People often want or need different things, and this can sometimes lead to **conflict**. A conflict is a disagreement or opposition of people's interests or ideas. Conflicts can occur in the workplace when one co-worker's wants or needs do not match another co-worker's wants or needs. Conflict can also happen between employees and their supervisors or customers. When such conflicts occur, it is important to acknowledge and deal with them effectively. Conflicts that are not resolved in a timely and appropriate manner may have a huge impact on a workplace's morale and productivity. However, when a conflict is clearly defined and successfully resolved, it can lead to positive changes.

In Real Life   The Almost Perfect Interview

Tina has been called to interview for a job she recently applied for. She is excited because she thinks this job could be a great fit for her. She passes the company's screening test, and everything goes smoothly at the interview.

The manager conducting the interview states that he wants to hire Tina, and he explains that the job will require her to work about 25–30 hours a week. Tina is upset because she really wants this job, but she knows she would need to work at least 35 hours a week to pay her bills. She wants to explain this to the manager, but she is not sure how to proceed.

 With a classmate, discuss the following questions. Share your ideas with the class.

1. What does Tina want?

2. What does the manager want?

3. How do you think Tina should handle this conflict?

Teacher Reminder
Review the teacher lesson at
www.mysteckvaughn.com/WORK

Causes of Conflict

In any workplace with more than one employee, success depends on working together as a team. Working together effectively can make a job fun and satisfying. But conflicts between co-workers can make a job difficult for everyone involved. Conflicts can arise between employees with:

- different goals or priorities,
- distinct styles, methods, or approaches to tasks, or
- opposing personalities.

Success in the workplace depends on being able to acknowledge these conflicts and bring them to a successful resolution.

 With a classmate, read the scenario and discuss the questions. Share your ideas with the class.

Victor and Luisa are salespeople at a clothing store. Every week they earn an hourly salary plus commission. Victor is very outgoing and is always talking to customers. He asks customers if they would like to try on different items and purchase matching accessories. Luisa is very quiet and less outgoing than Victor, but she is always polite and eager to help customers. Luisa and Victor get along, but sometimes Luisa feels that Victor takes potential customers away from her. Victor feels that Luisa is too passive and shouldn't blame him for not making sales.

4. How are Victor and Luisa the same? How are they different?

5. What is causing their conflict?

6. Is it easy for employees with different styles to work together? Why or why not?

Workplace Tip

When you acknowledge a workplace conflict, try to:

- Stay positive.
- Keep an open mind.
- See the conflict from the other person's point of view.

Why Acknowledge Conflict?

Conflict in the workplace can be stressful and difficult to handle. As a result, many employees choose to avoid conflict entirely. Rather than acknowledging it, they try one of these approaches:

- ***Ignoring*** "If I ignore the conflict, it will go away."
- ***Making Excuses*** "I have no time to deal with this right now."
- ***Underestimating*** "This problem is no big deal."

With a classmate, discuss the following questions. Share your ideas with the class.

7. Have you ever tried to avoid a conflict? What happened?

8. Why might employees try to ignore conflicts at work?

9. Do you think ignoring a workplace conflict is a good idea? Why or why not?

Develop Your Skills

Acknowledging a conflict is a necessary step toward the ultimate goal of resolving it. Use these strategies to help you acknowledge conflicts in your workplace.

Workplace Tip

When you define a conflict, remember:

- Do: Stay focused on the relevant facts.
- Don't: Make judgments about the people involved.

Define the Conflict

When you define a conflict clearly and **objectively**, you set yourself up for success to resolve it effectively. Put aside your emotions and any judgments about the other person or people involved in the situation. Try to see the conflict from another person's point of view. Then clearly and specifically identify the cause of the conflict.

 Read the scenario and answer the questions that follow.

Jan and Dave work at a busy café. At the last team meeting, their managers outlined a new end-of-day cleaning checklist. They explained that when every item on the checklist has been completed, all employees can clock out and go home.

Dave and Jan do not like working late, so they agree to clean different areas of the café to finish faster. After several evenings, Jan notices that Dave spends all of his time cleaning the espresso machines. Dave does a great job cleaning these machines, but Jan is angry because she must clean all of the other machines, wipe down tables, and mop the floors.

1. What is the conflict?

2. What is the cause of the conflict?

3. Should Jan acknowledge this conflict? Why or why not?

Identify Areas of Agreement and Disagreement

After you define the conflict, the next step is to identify areas of agreement and disagreement. This step will help you identify understandings or goals that both parties share. One strategy for organizing this information is to make a T-chart.

Discuss the T-chart with a classmate. Then answer the question.

Agree	Disagree
· Both Dave and Jan don't want to work late.	· Dave should spend all of his time cleaning the espresso machines.
· Dave and Jan should divide the work by cleaning different areas of the café.	· Jan should clean everything else.

4. How might this chart help Dave and Jan solve their conflict?

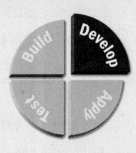

Read the scenario and answer the questions that follow.

Yolanda and Toby are activity aides at a children's rehabilitation center. They both enjoy interacting with children and helping them get well. On Tuesdays Toby's group is scheduled to use the playroom after Yolanda's group. Toby is frustrated because every Tuesday he enters the playroom and finds that the games and puzzles are a mess.

5. What is the conflict?

6. What common goal do the employees share?

Restate the Conflict

Once you understand the conflict, its causes, and areas of agreement and disagreement, you should restate the conflict in your own words. Restating the conflict to yourself is a good way to confirm that you understand it. Restating it to the person you are having a conflict with is the first step to finding a solution that you are both happy with.

When you restate a conflict, it is important to be objective. It is not the time to take sides or make **accusations**. Doing so will only hurt your chances of resolving the conflict. Choose your words carefully and use details and examples to support your explanation.

Read the following accusations and restate the conflicts objectively. Remember to support your statements with details and examples.

7. "Dave, you are always slacking off on your closing duties!"

8. "Dr. Punjabi, Yolanda always leaves a huge mess in the playroom."

When people refuse to acknowledge workplace conflicts, strong emotions such as anger, disappointment, frustration, and anxiety can build over time like a volcano waiting to erupt. Recognizing and acknowledging conflicts as they arise can keep that volcano under control and prevent minor workplace issues from turning into major ones.

| GOT IT? | Recognizing and acknowledging conflicts will help you resolve workplace issues. To acknowledge a conflict: |

- Define the conflict clearly and objectively.
- Identify areas of agreement and disagreement.
- Restate the conflict using details and examples.

To-Do List
Remember to follow these steps when applying your knowledge:

❑ **Define the conflict**

❑ **Identify areas of agreement and disagreement**

❑ **Restate the conflict**

Apply Your Knowledge

Resolving a conflict in the workplace requires that you define it clearly, identify areas of agreement and disagreement, and restate the conflict.

As you read the following scenarios, think about what you have learned in this lesson about conflict. Select what you think is the best response and the worst response to each situation.

1. Marc just began working as a receptionist at a dentist's office. One of the dentists, Dr. Otto, is very friendly and always stops to greet Marc and ask him about his family and friends. Another dentist, Dr. Miller, rarely speaks to Marc. Dr. Miller often grabs forms off of Marc's desk and walks away without saying a word. This behavior bothers Marc. What should Marc do?

    A. Tell Dr. Otto about his problem.

    B. Politely approach Dr. Miller about the issue.

    C. Do nothing and hope that Dr. Miller changes.

    D. Ask Dr. Otto to talk to Dr. Miller.

Best Answer		Worst Answer	

2. One afternoon you are in the break room eating your lunch. Your co-worker Jill is sitting at a table nearby chatting on her cell phone. She is talking loudly, and you hear her making rude comments and jokes about Noel, the person who sits in the cube next to yours. What should you do?

    A. Calmly confront Jill and ask her to refrain from making rude comments.

    B. Demand that your co-worker hang up her phone immediately.

    C. Ignore Jill, leave the break room, and go eat lunch at your desk.

    D. E-mail Noel a list of Jill's rude comments and jokes.

Best Answer		Worst Answer	

3. Maria and Kurt work at a grocery store. One morning their manager, Mr. Tevez, explains that some new products have arrived and that the store's shelves will need to be reorganized. To prepare for this reorganization, Mr. Tevez asks Maria and Kurt to work together to clean all of the shelves in the frozen foods section. As Maria is finishing cleaning the shelves in one aisle, she notices that Kurt has cleaned only one shelf and is sitting down taking a break. What should Maria do?

A. Clean the remaining shelves herself.

B. Ask Mr. Tevez to fire Kurt.

C. Tell another co-worker to help her clean.

D. Talk to Kurt and create a cleaning plan.

Best Answer		Worst Answer	

In Real Life   Put Your Skills to Work!

You work at a car rental agency. One of your jobs is to enter the vehicle return paperwork into the computer system. One day your co-worker, Mike, is talking to a customer who is dropping off a car. After the customer pays, Mike leaves for lunch. You begin to enter the paperwork into the computer and discover that Mike has not filled out the gas and mileage portions of the form. This is the second time this has happened.

Think about the problem you are facing and put your skills to work! How would you acknowledge this conflict?

Think About It!

What conflicts exist in your workplace?

How can acknowledging a conflict help you resolve it?

Your ability to define and solve conflicts at work can help you in all types of situations. Acknowledging these conflicts, although difficult at times, will help you recognize their causes and identify constructive ways to resolve them. Ignoring a conflict or denying that it exists can cause tension and actually make the conflict worse.

Workplace Tip

When faced with this conflict, did you think about:

• Defining the conflict?

• Identifying areas of agreement and disagreement?

• How to restate the conflict?

Answer Key

1. The best answer is B. Politely approaching Dr. Miller about the issue is a good step toward resolving the conflict. The worst answer is C. Doing nothing and hoping that Dr. Miller will change does not acknowledge or define the conflict.

2. The best answer is A. Calmly confronting your co-worker is a good way to acknowledge the conflict. The worst answer is D. E-mailing the co-worker who is being made fun of does not acknowledge the conflict with Jill and will likely make the situation worse.

3. The best answer is D. Talking to Kurt and creating a cleaning plan acknowledges the conflict and takes action to resolve it. The worst answer is B. Asking the manager to fire Kurt is not a reasonable way to respond to the conflict.

Test Your WRC Skills

Select the best response and the worst response to each situation.

1. You work in a busy office. Everyone in the office shares one copy machine. Every time you use the copy machine after your co-worker Alex, there is no paper in it. How should you handle this situation?

Best	Worst	
○	○	Check the copy machine each morning to make sure it has paper.
○	○	Tell your supervisor that Alex never refills the copy machine's paper.
○	○	Make all of your copies after Alex leaves for the day.
○	○	Ask Alex to refill the copy machine if he uses all the paper.

2. The warehouse where you work has several pallets that must be moved before this afternoon's shipment arrives. Your supervisor makes an announcement asking all employees who are certified to operate forklifts to help move the pallets. You see Paul, a new employee, begin to drive a forklift toward one of the pallets. You know that Paul is not certified to operate a forklift. How should you handle this situation?

Best	Worst	
○	○	Tell a co-worker who is certified to operate a forklift to help you move the pallets.
○	○	Tell Paul to drive the forklift slowly and carefully so he can avoid accidents.
○	○	Stop Paul and explain why it is unsafe for uncertified workers to operate forklifts.
○	○	Ask your supervisor to review the warehouse safety procedures at your next meeting.

3. You know that your co-worker is not happy with her commute or her current salary. One day you see her filling out online job applications at work. The next day you hear her calling to schedule interviews for jobs at other companies. How should you handle this situation?

Best	Worst	
○	○	Do nothing and hope that your manager catches your co-worker while she is looking up other jobs.
○	○	Meet with your co-workers to complain about the current salaries that you are earning.
○	○	Explain to your co-worker that she could get in trouble for using her work phone and computer to apply for other jobs.
○	○	Tell your co-worker that she should be happy with her current salary and not complain.

4. You work at a deli located near a big university. Your manager has just posted a sign that says "Every Wednesday: 50% Discount for Students with Valid ID Card." One afternoon a customer comes in and orders a sandwich. When you are ringing up the order, she asks for a student discount. You ask to see her ID. She says she never shows her ID card when she buys a sandwich. How should you handle this situation?

Best	Worst	
○	○	Ask a co-worker to ring up the customer.
○	○	Calmly explain the policy and point out the sign.
○	○	Tell the customer not to come back to the deli again.
○	○	Give the customer a coupon for a free sandwich.

5. Your company just relocated to a new building, and you have a new cubicle. You are happy because this workspace has a window and a new desk. However, the cubicle walls are thinner than the ones in the old building, and you can hear everything that is going on around you. One of your managers has the office closest to your workspace. He always has his door open, and he talks loudly whenever he makes a phone call. How should you handle this situation?

Best	Worst	
○	○	Request to move to a cubical near a quiet manager.
○	○	Slam your manager's door shut whenever he is being loud.
○	○	Kindly ask your manager to close his door when he makes calls.
○	○	Complain to your co-workers about the new building.

6. You are a scheduling assistant at a doctor's office. Part of your job is to call each patient two days before an appointment to confirm it. When you make these calls, you also explain that patients will be charged a $25 rescheduling fee if they fail to give notice 24 hours before canceling an appointment. Today a patient calls and says she is frustrated because there is a $25 rescheduling fee on her bill even though she rescheduled two days before her appointment. How should you handle this situation?

Best	Worst	
○	○	Apologize for the error and tell the patient that you will correct the charges on her bill.
○	○	Inform the patient that there is nothing you can do and hang up the phone.
○	○	Complain to your co-workers about the call log and rescheduling fee procedures.
○	○	Tell the patient you will charge her less the next time she needs to reschedule.

Check your answers on page 164.

Active Listening

Build on What You Know

Have you ever been explaining your point of view and felt that the person you were speaking to wasn't listening? How did you feel? Active listening is always useful, but it is especially important during a conflict. In fact, not listening can actually make a conflict worse.

Active listening during a conflict requires a lot of concentration because anger or frustration can distract you. It is important that you stop thinking about what you will say next, put aside your emotions, and focus on what the speaker is saying. If you use listening strategies to identify and follow a speaker's main points, you can identify the cause of the conflict and figure out what is needed to resolve it.

Develop Your Skills

Use these strategies to help you listen actively during a conflict:

- Watch and listen for **social cues,** such as the speaker's tone of voice, gestures, and other body language.
- Listen for signal words and phrases that indicate order, cause and effect, or main points.
- Try to figure out the meaning of unfamiliar words. If you don't know the meaning, ask the speaker.

Role-play the following situation with a fellow classmate. Remember to listen carefully for clues that will help you identify and follow the main points of the conversation. Complete your role-play by discussing the following questions.

The store where you work has just been remodeled. A customer comes to you waving his shopping list in the air. He starts yelling: *I can't find anything in this store! First, I walked to the pharmacy and found that it's the new electronics department. When I asked where the pain medications are, a cashier sent me way across the store to aisle twelve. Then I went to look for toiletries, and I ended up lost near the restrooms! I used to enjoy shopping here, but now I need a map to help me find each item on my list!*

1. What social cues tell you that the customer is unhappy?

2. What is the problem from the customer's point of view?

3. What signal words help you identify the customer's main points?

4. Based on what you know, what is the best way to respond to this conflict?

Essential Tasks

Use strategies and resources (e.g., context clues, graphics, word parts, dictionary, other people) to define unfamiliar words, phrases, and idioms

Recognize predictable rhetorical structures (e.g., main idea, supporting detail, Q&A, chronology, stepped instructions, cause and effect) that guide listening

Recognize conventions in verbal communications (e.g., signal words, opening and closing discourse, shift) that signal sequence and transitions in topic or type of discourse

Recognize and respond to social cues (e.g., speaker's need for validation, speaker's comprehension checks, opportunities to take the floor, end of conversation) in conversation

Develop Your Skills Answer Key

1. Waving his shopping list; yelling

2. It is difficult to find what he needs because of the store's new layout.

3. *First, when, then, but*

4. Apologize for the inconvenience and offer to help the customer find the remaining items on his list.

Apply Your Knowledge

Read the following scenario and answer the questions.

Your cabinet company is behind on a big project, and several co-workers have volunteered for extra shifts in order to make the deadline. One night after her shift ends, a co-worker named Irma rolls her eyes and says: *I can't believe we're all working so hard to finish this stupid project. The deadline is a joke. Even if we expedite the shipping, the cabinets still won't get to the building site in time. And on top of that, I'm sick of having to work extra shifts when that lazy Dennis never has to work late. All he has to say is, "I have to pick up my kids," and presto! No work! I have half a mind to follow him home and see if he has any kids at all!*

5. What social cues reveal that Irma is upset?

6. What is the meaning of the word *expedite*?

7. What are two conflicts that Irma has?

8. Does Irma expect you to solve her problems? Explain.

9. Based on what you know, what is the best way to respond to this conflict?

Test Your WRC Skills Scenario 8

Listen to hear a conversation between two co-workers. You may listen to the conversation more than once before answering the question.

Active Listening Scenarios are available at www.mysteckvaughn.com/WORK.

Based on the conversation, what is the meaning of the phrase "cut corners"?

A. Help factories save energy

B. Do some tasks but not others

C. Trim the sides of large objects

D. Attend safety training

Check your answer on page 164.

Apply Your Knowledge **Answer Key**

5. She rolls her eyes and uses strong language to express her frustration.

6. To speed up

7. She does not like having to work so hard, and she also resents Dennis for not working extra shifts.

8. No. If Irma were looking for solutions, she would express herself in a different way and probably ask for help. Irma's complaints are more likely an attempt to get sympathy from you.

9. Possible answer: Agree that the situation is frustrating but gently remind Irma that the extra shifts are voluntary.

Resolve Conflict

Essential Tasks

Generate options for resolving the conflict that have a win/win potential

Negotiate an agreement that will satisfy the conflicted parties using a range of strategies to facilitate negotiation

Negotiate an agreement that will satisfy the conflicted parties by monitoring the process for its effectiveness and fairness

Build on What You Know

Have you ever kept quiet about something that really bothered you? Perhaps you left a hair salon with a bad haircut because you didn't want to offend the stylist by asking her to fix it. Or maybe you silently resented a friend because he wanted to stay home and play games, but you wanted to go to the movies. On the other hand, maybe you didn't keep your emotions inside at all. Instead, you let them out in a burst of anger. You insulted the hairstylist in front of the entire store or accused your friend of being selfish. These are all excellent examples of how *not* to resolve a conflict.

Conflict is an unavoidable part of both your personal and work life. However, how you deal with it makes all the difference. Learning to resolve conflict successfully will improve your relationships with friends and family, as well as co-workers, customers, and supervisors. This lesson will teach you how to effectively resolve conflicts in the workplace.

In Real Life   Conflict Catastrophe

Felix's frustration with his co-worker, Sandy, has been increasing over the past few weeks. Sandy takes several long breaks each day. The manager at the store where Felix and Sandy work has not noticed Sandy's absences and has been giving Felix more work because unfinished tasks around the store are building up.

One day, as Sandy is leaving for yet another break, Felix becomes enraged. He yells at Sandy and calls her lazy. He accuses her of avoiding work and not caring about the fact that he has to take on extra tasks. He threatens to tell the manager if she keeps taking lengthy breaks. Then Felix storms off angrily before Sandy can speak.

 With a classmate, discuss the following questions. Share your ideas with the class.

1. How would you have felt if you were Felix? If you were Sandy?

2. Did Felix handle the situation well? Why or why not?

3. What do you think will result from Felix's outburst?

4. How would you have handled this situation?

Teacher Reminder
Review the teacher lesson at
www.mysteckvaughn.com/WORK

What is Conflict Resolution?

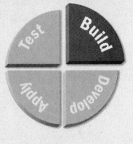

In Lesson 5, you learned that conflict happens when someone wants or needs something that goes against what somebody else wants or needs. Conflict can happen between individuals or groups, and it can take many forms. Once conflict occurs and is acknowledged, however, it can be handled in different ways.

You've learned there are some very poor ways to deal with conflict. Avoiding conflict or letting emotions control your behavior only lead to more conflict. These reactions often cause hostility and negative attitudes. Luckily, there are positive ways to respond to conflict. **Conflict resolution** is the process of solving a disagreement. When done successfully, it can lead to respect, understanding, and a better outcome for all the people involved.

Think about how conflicts you have experienced have ended. Fill in the following chart and answer the questions below. Discuss your responses with the class.

A time I *did* get what I wanted after a disagreement was . . .	A time I *didn't* get what I wanted after a disagreement was . . .
I felt . . .	I felt . . .
The other person or people felt . . .	The other person or people felt . . .
I would/wouldn't handle the disagreement differently now because . . .	I would/wouldn't handle the disagreement differently now because . . .

> **Workplace Tip**
>
> You may think people are satisfied with the outcome of a conflict when they are not. People may also say that they are pleased with a solution when they really feel otherwise. Good communication can prevent these situations from happening.

5. How do you generally resolve your conflicts?

6. Do you usually feel better or worse after a conflict is over? Why?

7. How do you think you could improve your conflict resolution skills?

Develop Your Skills

Being able to successfully resolve conflicts will make your interactions at work more enjoyable and productive. So how is it done? Read and practice the following strategies to help you the next time you face a conflict in the workplace.

Generate Options

Once you have acknowledged that there is a conflict, think about how you want to approach it. What are your options? How can you resolve the conflict? This is the point when you can decide to handle the conflict effectively or poorly.

The options you come up with will ultimately lead to a solution in one of the following categories:

Win-Win	Win-Lose
Both people get something they want or need.	You get something you want or need, but the other person does not.
Lose-Win	**Lose-Lose**
The other person gets something he or she wants or needs, but you do not.	Neither person gets what they want or need.

Only options that could lead to a win-win solution will resolve your conflict. This is because a conflict is not truly resolved until everyone is satisfied with the outcome.

 Read the following conflict. Then identify if the options are likely to produce a win-win solution. Discuss with a classmate why or why not.

It is your job to install new kitchen windows in the house your construction company is renovating. Andy, another worker, was supposed to remove the old windows, but he thinks his other tasks are more important. You are frustrated because you can't do your work until Andy takes out the old windows.

1. You could talk to Andy and try to come up with a solution that works for both of you.

2. You could not do your task and keep bothering Andy to remove the old windows.

3. You could feel angry at Andy but not say anything, and remove the old windows yourself.

Negotiate a Win-Win Solution

Options that will lead to a win-win solution usually involve speaking with the person you are having a conflict with to **negotiate** a solution. When you negotiate, you work together to find a win-win solution.

Talking to the person you are having a disagreement with is not something most people enjoy doing. It can be challenging because you may feel strongly about the issue or frustrated with the other person. Use the following tips to help you work successfully with others to find a solution that works for you both.

- **Be calm and objective.** Don't try to speak to the person if you are upset. Give yourself time to calm down before trying to find a solution.

- **Focus on the problem.** Separate the problem from the person. Explain the problem objectively without making accusations. Use details and examples to make your explanation clear.

- **Listen to the other person.** Listen to the other person's position on the issue. Do not interrupt.

- **Discuss options.** Try to find a solution in which you both get something you want or need. Recognize that it may not be possible for both people to get everything they want. You may need to **compromise** to come up with the best solution.

Once you find a win-win solution that is fair and possible, put it into practice. Check to make sure the solution is working. If you need to, negotiate a new solution.

Role-play these scenarios with a classmate. First, do not follow any of the tips listed above. Then practice using the tips to resolve the conflict.

4. Vince is frustrated because his co-worker Marcus has been taking more than his share of money from the tip jar.

5. During a performance review, Nicole disagrees with the negative feedback her supervisor gives her about her work performance.

Workplace Tip

When you compromise, discuss the following questions:

- What is the goal of the compromise?
- What are you both willing and not willing to give up?
- How will the outcome affect everyone involved?

Answer Key

1. Likely to produce a win-win solution because both people involved can communicate their needs and discuss possible solutions that will benefit them both
2. Unlikely to produce a win-win solution because Andy may become annoyed and may not help you
3. Unlikely to produce a win-win solution because you will have to do extra work and will continue to feel angry with Andy
4. Answers will vary, but students should use the tips they learned to resolve the conflict.
5. Answers will vary, but students should use the tips they learned to resolve the conflict.

GOT IT? | **Workplace conflicts happen to everyone. You can resolve a conflict successfully if you:**

- Acknowledge the conflict rather than avoid it.
- Think of ways to approach the conflict that could lead to a win-win solution.
- Negotiate a win-win solution in a calm, fair way.
- Make sure that the solution you decide on works, and if needed, find a better solution.

To-Do List

Remember to follow these steps when applying your knowledge:

❑ **Generate options**

❑ **Negotiate a win-win solution**

❑ **Compromise if necessary**

❑ **Make sure the solution works**

Apply Your Knowledge

Resolving workplace conflicts requires you to apply a variety of strategies that will help you achieve a win-win solution.

As you read the following scenarios, think about how you could effectively resolve the conflict. Select what you think is the best response and the worst response to each situation.

1. You are upset because your co-worker, Ali, assumes you will cover her shifts at the warehouse when she is out of town next week. You like Ali, and she covered your shifts when you were on vacation last month. You are available to work the shifts, but you feel that Ali should have asked you before telling the manager that you would be covering for her. What should you do?

   A. Tell Ali you will cover for her, but request that next time she ask you first.

   B. Ask the manager to find someone else to cover Ali's shifts.

   C. Don't say anything to Ali and cover her shifts since you are available.

   D. Assure Ali you will cover her shifts and then don't show up.

Best Answer		Worst Answer	

2. Your friend has been unemployed for a few months and has been asking you to put in a good word for him at the landscaping company where you work. Though he doesn't have any experience, you convince the owner to hire him. You have a good reputation, and the owner trusts your judgment. The first week your friend is on the job, he shows up late and leaves early. He hardly works and doesn't do the tasks he is supposed to do correctly. You fear that his behavior is making you look bad. What should you do?

   A. Don't do anything and hope that his behavior improves next week.

   B. Tell the owner that you regret recommending your friend and request that he be fired immediately.

   C. Explain to your friend that he needs to put more effort into his work or you will report him to the owner.

   D. Ask another worker to find out why your friend is not taking work seriously.

Best Answer		Worst Answer	

One of your responsibilities at the pizza shop where you work is to take orders over the phone. A customer calls and orders a large sausage pizza to pick up. When he arrives, he insists that he ordered a large pepperoni pizza. You try to explain that you are sure he ordered sausage, but he becomes very angry. He demands that you fix the problem or he will complain to the manager about your poor service. You are very upset by the way the customer is treating you. Customers are usually very pleased when you help them.

Think about the problem you are facing and put your skills to work! How should you approach the conflict? What strategies can you use?

Think About It!

Do you often have conflicts with the same people? Why or why not?

In what ways will you handle conflicts differently than you used to?

Conflicts with co-workers, supervisors, clients, or customers are not uncommon in the workplace and can be caused by all kinds of issues. The conflicts may be short-lived and easy to resolve, or they might be emotionally charged and confrontational. No matter what the conflicts are, how you react can greatly influence the outcome. If you use the strategies you learned in this lesson, you will be able to find solutions that benefit everybody involved. And that's something no one will want to argue with!

Workplace Tip

When resolving the conflict, did you think about:

- Options that would ultimately lead to a win-win solution?
- Negotiating a win-win solution using the conflict resolution tips?
- Making sure the solution resolved the conflict?

Answer Key

1. The best answer is A. Expressing your feelings and politely communicating how you would like to handle such situations will help you maintain your relationship with your co-worker and set clear expectations for the future. The worst answer is D. It is deceitful to tell someone that you will do something and then not do it. Your relationship with your co-worker will likely be damaged, and the company will be short workers because of your irresponsibility.

2. The best answer is C. Confronting your friend and giving him the chance to correct his poor behavior before reporting him is the best course of action. The worst answer is B. Going to the owner and asking for your friend to be fired damages your relationship with your friend, doesn't give your friend a chance to improve his behavior, and leaves the owner short a worker if he does decide to fire him.

Test Your WRC Skills

Select the best response and the worst response to each situation.

1. It is 5:00 P.M. and you are closing the gift shop where you work. Just as you turn the sign to "Closed," a customer comes to the door and explains that tomorrow is her nephew's birthday. She tells you that she really wants to buy him a present from your store and thought the store was open until 5:30. How should you handle this situation?

Best	Worst	
○	○	Explain that you are closing, but the customer can make a quick purchase if she knows what she wants to buy.
○	○	Recommend that the customer come back at 8:00 A.M. when the gift shop reopens.
○	○	Suggest that the customer look for a gift at another gift shop that is open later.
○	○	Let the customer come in to shop for a gift while you close and balance the cash register.

2. A co-worker decides to listen to her radio at work because it keeps her alert. You cannot concentrate with the music playing. How should you handle this situation?

Best	Worst	
○	○	Bring in a radio and play it really loud so your co-worker knows how annoying it is.
○	○	Suggest that your co-worker use headphones when she listens to the radio at work.
○	○	Complain about the music to your other co-workers and see if they have any ideas.
○	○	Tell your co-worker that she is being inconsiderate and to stop playing the music.

3. You are the assistant manager at an electronics store. Roberto, one of the employees, has asked for extra shifts to help him pay some unexpected expenses. You know that the other employees will be upset if you take away any of their hours. How should you handle this situation?

Best	Worst	
○	○	Suggest that Roberto look for a second job.
○	○	Ask Roberto to fill in for employees who need their shifts covered.
○	○	Have Roberto convince the other employees to give up some hours.
○	○	Give Roberto the extra shifts he needs until he pays off the expenses.

4. One of the residents at the nursing home where you work has been disrupting the other residents by staying up late watching TV. He must turn up the volume because he has poor hearing, but the noise keeps other residents awake, and they are becoming angry. You know this resident has trouble sleeping and that he finds comfort in watching old shows. How should you handle this situation?

Best	Worst	
○	○	Alternate between nights the resident can watch TV and nights he can't.
○	○	Tell the resident he can't watch TV past 7:00 P.M. because he is disturbing too many people.
○	○	Allow the resident to watch TV in a community room away from the rooms where the other residents sleep.
○	○	Let the resident continue to watch TV but with the volume turned down lower.

5. You are a delivery driver for a restaurant. You are frustrated because you seem to be assigned all the deliveries that are on the outskirts of town. Because you have to drive so far, you make fewer deliveries than the other drivers. This means that you also make less money in tips. You have already asked the other drivers to leave some of the closer deliveries for you, but they haven't done so. How should you handle this situation?

Best	Worst	
○	○	Propose that the drivers split tips equally so that it is in everybody's best interest to make as many deliveries as possible.
○	○	Ask the manager to make sure you get some deliveries that are closer to the restaurant.
○	○	Speed on your way to make the deliveries so that you can try to make more deliveries.
○	○	Complain to the other workers in the restaurant about how unfair the delivery assignments are.

6. You work as an office clerk at an accounting firm. Jane, a co-worker with whom you share an office, is sneaking glances of your e-mails over your shoulder. This has been a problem for several weeks. You have already asked her politely to respect your privacy. How should you handle this situation?

Best	Worst	
○	○	Tell other co-workers about how inconsiderate Jane is.
○	○	Only check your e-mail when Jane is out of the office.
○	○	Start reading Jane's e-mail over her shoulder.
○	○	Ask your supervisor if you can move to a different desk.

Check your answers on page 165.

Workplace Tip

Be aware of the social cues you are projecting as you listen. Face the speaker, make eye contact, and nod to show that you understand what they are saying.

Develop Your Skills Answer Key

1. The co-worker is showing that he is upset, but he is not communicating the reasons why.

2. The co-worker can speak to you in a calm tone and explain the problem.

Active Listening

Build on What You Know

How do you know if someone is upset with you? Does the person avoid you? Maybe the person yells and points their finger at you in an accusing way. These are examples of social cues that can occur during a conflict.

Social cues are one way people communicate their feelings. They can include body language, facial expressions, as well as volume and tone of voice. Social cues are useful because they give you information about what others are thinking. Sometimes, however, they can prevent good communication. This is especially true during conflict. It's certainly not easy to talk to a co-worker if he or she refuses to make eye contact or speaks in a quick, harsh tone. Seeking clarification of the other person's point of view is an effective way to respond to conflict-related social cues in the workplace.

Develop Your Skills

Use these steps to recognize and respond to social cues related to conflict.

- **Recognize** Notice how someone stands, looks at you, and speaks to you to determine how they feel about the conflict.

- **Communicate** Tell the person that their behavior lets you know that they are upset, but not necessarily why or what they need from you. Request that the person calmly and clearly explain the problem.

- **Listen and Respond** Listen to the other person's point of view. Use statements such as "I understand that . . ." and "What I hear you saying is . . ." to show that you value what they say and to confirm your own understanding. If you don't understand, ask them to repeat or clarify. You might ask them to slow their speech or use different words so that you can understand better.

Role-play the following situation. Then discuss the questions.

A co-worker has been ignoring you lately and you don't know why. You say: *I've noticed you haven't been speaking to me lately, and I'm wondering if there is something wrong. I can't fix what is wrong if I don't understand what the problem is. Would you be willing to talk about it over lunch?*

1. How does your co-worker's behavior prevent you from understanding the conflict?

2. How can the co-worker communicate the problem more effectively?

Apply Your Knowledge

Read the following scenario and answer the questions.

A hotel guest stomps up to the front desk where you work and slams down a room service bill on the counter. His speaks loudly and quickly as he declares: *This bill is outrageous! Are you kidding me? I'm not made of money! Why don't you put your prices on the menu? If I had known you were going to charge so much I would have taken my business somewhere else. I can't believe you people! It's not like this is a five star hotel!*

3. What are some social cues that tell you how the guest feels?

4. What tone should you use to tell to the guest that you need him to explain the problem calmly and clearly?

5. How can you show the guest that you understand his position?

6. What could you say to clear up any confusion about why the customer is upset by the bill?

Test Your WRC Skills Scenario 9

 **Listen to hear a conversation between two co-workers. You may listen to the conversation more than once before answering the question.**

Active Listening Scenarios are available at www.mysteckvaughn.com/WORK.

Which of the following BEST describes the tone of the speaker?

A. Sad

B. Pleased

C. Angry

D. Confused

Check your answer on page 165.

To-Do List

Remember to follow these steps when applying your knowledge:

❑ **Recognize social cues**

❑ **Communicate openly**

❑ **Listen and respond**

Apply Your Knowledge **Answer Key**

3. Stomping, slamming the bill down, speaking loudly and quickly

4. A calm and clear tone

5. Possible answer: Use "I" messages to show that you understand what the guest is saying and that you care about the problem. Social cues such as eye contact, facing the guest, and nodding also demonstrate that you are listening.

6. Possible answer: "Can you please explain which charges are a problem?"

Skills for the Workplace

Recognize Barriers

Have you ever been listening to someone speak, and you just can't understand him or her no matter how hard you try? Perhaps your doctor speaks with a heavy accent, or your teacher uses a lot of words you do not understand. These kinds of barriers to communication happen in the workplace, too. Effective communication depends on recognizing the barriers that exist and figuring out how to work around them.

Communication barriers come in many forms:

- **Language** Some co-workers and customers may not speak English. *Strategies for clarification:* If you will need to communicate often with speakers of other languages, try to learn some key words and phrases. Use gestures, maps, and pictures to help you communicate.

- **Lack of knowledge or resources** You may not understand the words a speaker uses or have the background knowledge or experience you need to understand the information. *Strategies for clarification:* Ask questions that will help you understand. You could also ask the person to show you how to do something rather than explaining it with words.

- **Emotions and stress** The emotions of both the speaker and the listener can get in the way of effective communication. *Strategies for clarification:* Restate what you heard and allow the speaker to correct any misunderstandings. It is often helpful to come back to the topic at a later time when your emotions have calmed.

Workplace Tip
Visual aids can help people overcome many different communication barriers. If you have an idea for a helpful map, chart, or diagram, create a draft and show your manager. Your initiative will be appreciated!

Workplace Scenario

Sandra just got a job at the front desk of a hotel. Sandra knows some Spanish, but not enough to have a conversation at work. A hotel guest comes up to Sandra and asks a question. Sandra thinks she understands the words for *where* and *museum*.

1. What is the barrier between Sandra and the hotel guest? *Sandra and the guest speak different languages.*

2. How could Sandra work around this communication barrier? *She could ask a bilingual co-worker to translate, or she could use a map to guide the guest to a nearby museum.*

Workplace Practice

You are in a day-long training session for new employees. It is one hour before the end of the session, and a representative from the Human Resources department is giving a long presentation about all the benefits available at the company. You made it through all his explanations of the health insurance benefits just fine, but now the representative is talking about 401K plans, matching funds, vesting, and many other financial concepts you do not have any experience with. You find yourself getting frustrated and wishing the presentation would end so you can get on with your day.

1. What are the communication barriers in this situation?

2. What could you do to address these barriers?

3. Why might it be important to address the communication barriers in this situation?

One communication barrier in this situation is that you lack the background knowledge to understand what the representative is saying. Another barrier is your frustration, which makes it more difficult for you to understand the information. To overcome these barriers, you should ask the representative to explain the unfamiliar terms. Once you understand the basics, you will feel less frustrated and be able to understand the rest of the information better. If you do not ask, you could end up losing out on important retirement benefits, including contributions from your company.

It's Your Turn!

1. You work as a sales representative at a cell phone store. A customer wants to know the difference between two cell phone plans. When you start to explain each plan, you notice that the customer looks confused. What might help you overcome this communication barrier?

2. You work at the information desk at the local library. Someone asks you in Spanish where the children's books are located. You understand the question but do not know enough Spanish to answer the question. None of your co-workers can speak Spanish. How should you handle this situation?

3. You have a job as a clerk at a hospital. At a meeting, your co-workers and managers used many words and phrases that were unfamiliar to you. Now you are unsure how you should proceed with one of your assignments. How should you handle this situation?

It's Your Turn! Answer Key

1. Possible answer: A list or chart showing the cell phone plans and their features would provide additional support to help the customer understand.

2. You could take the guest to the section where the children's books are located or show the guest a library map and point to the location.

3. You can tell a co-worker or your manager that you didn't understand something from the meeting and ask for clarification.

Chapter 3 Assessment

Select the best response and the worst response to each situation.

1. You have been assigned to complete a tiling job at a client's home. Your manager says you should try to finish the job in five hours. When you get to the client's home, the client explains that she wants the job done in three hours. How should you handle this situation?

Best	Worst	
○	○	Rush to finish the job in three hours to please the client, even if you can't do your best work.
○	○	Begin working and take as long as you need to finish the job since you want to do a good job.
○	○	Tell your manager that the client's request conflicts with the instructions you were given.
○	○	Tell your manager that you won't do the job because you don't like the client's attitude.

2. At the nursing home where you work, you hear one of the attendants speaking rudely to one of the elderly residents. Even though you understand the attendant is under a lot of stress, you know that this behavior is unacceptable. How should you handle this situation?

Best	Worst	
○	○	Ignore the behavior and hope that it will eventually stop or that a supervisor will talk to the attendant.
○	○	Confront the attendant and tell him that you know the job is stressful but he should always be respectful.
○	○	Ask other co-workers what they think you should do about the attendant's behavior.
○	○	Explain to the nursing home residents why some attendants are under a lot of stress.

3. At the hotel where you work, customers have been complaining of dirty rooms. Your manager thinks the cleaning staff is not working hard enough, but you think the problem is ineffective scheduling that causes the cleaning staff to rush through each room. How should you handle this situation?

Best	Worst	
○	○	Reschedule the cleaning staff without consulting with your manager.
○	○	Let the manager solve the problem since she is more experienced.
○	○	Tell the cleaning staff they need to work harder.
○	○	Tell your manager why you think the schedule is causing the problem.

4. You work as a pharmacy aide, and a co-worker named Mery has been calling in sick a lot. Your supervisor says he is considering firing Mery if she cannot produce a doctor's note to prove she was sick. How should you handle this situation?

Best	Worst	
○	○	Don't contact Mery—it's her responsibility to get the doctor's note on her own.
○	○	Tell your supervisor that you are friends with Mery and know that she has medical problems.
○	○	Call Mery and let her know that she needs to get a doctor's note to prove she is sick.
○	○	During your lunch break, ask your co-workers if they think Mery is really sick.

5. You are in charge of stocking the office supply room at a small legal office. Some of the employees prefer pens that cost $1.50 each; other employees think that $1.50 is too much to spend on a pen. How should you handle this situation?

Best	Worst	
○	○	Order the expensive pens for all the employees because they are the best quality.
○	○	Tell the staff to bring their own pens because you don't want to deal with the problem.
○	○	Order the cheaper pens because they are the most cost effective for the company.
○	○	Order the more expensive pens for the employees who want them and the cheaper pens for everyone else.

6. You work at a restaurant, and two co-workers named Eric and Sara are arguing. Eric thinks he has to clean up more large messes than Sara. How should you handle this situation?

Best	Worst	
○	○	Suggest to your co-workers that whoever finds the mess should clean it.
○	○	Stay out of their disagreement because you don't want to get involved.
○	○	Tell your manager that Eric and Sara are fighting about who should clean up messes.
○	○	Suggest that Eric and Sara keep a log of who cleans large messes and when.

7. You work at an interior design firm, and your manager will be hiring several contractors for upcoming projects. A contractor calls you and says he would like to be considered for a particular project, but he doesn't have the necessary experience. How should you handle this situation?

Best	Worst	
○	○	Tell the contractor there aren't any upcoming projects that he is qualified for.
○	○	Tell the contractor he can have the job if he learns the necessary skills in two weeks.
○	○	Assign the contractor to the project anyway and hope he picks the skills up as he goes along.
○	○	Analyze the contractor's strengths and experience and try to match him with a project that fits his abilities.

8. Your company uses the following sign when floors are wet and slippery. You see your co-worker Travis running through the hall with a large container of sharp tools. How should you handle this situation?

CAUTION

Best	Worst	
○	○	Point to the sign and explain to Travis that he could slip and hurt himself.
○	○	Yell at Travis to stop running because it's not allowed.
○	○	Don't stop Travis because he should know not to run in this area.
○	○	Ask people who mop to use larger signs to indicate that the floors are wet.

9. A large shipment of merchandise just arrived at the warehouse where you work. Your supervisor wants the merchandise to be stocked by the end of the day. Two employees are scheduled to leave in 15 minutes, and you are scheduled to leave in one hour and 15 minutes. You will not be able to complete the task on time without help. How should you handle this situation?

Best	Worst	
○	○	Ask the two employees nicely if they could work a little late to help stock the merchandise.
○	○	Call the merchandise company and yell at them for sending the shipment late in the day.
○	○	Ask your supervisor to demand the two employees stay and help.
○	○	Work extra hours to make sure the merchandise is stocked on time.

Scenario 10

Listen to hear a segment about a company policy about computer use. You may listen to the segment more than once before answering the questions.

Active Listening Scenarios are available at www.mysteckvaughn.com/WORK.

10. What is the main idea that the speaker expresses to Karen?

    A. Using a company computer to send personal e-mails is not allowed.

    B. Karen can shop for items on her computer during her lunch break.

    C. Karen can keep using her computer to shop online at work.

    D. Using a company computer to shop online is against company policy.

11. Which of the following **BEST** describes the tone of the speaker?

    A. Overly cheerful

    B. Friendly but firm

    C. Bored and uninterested

    D. Aggressive and hostile

12. What might Karen say if she wants to clear up confusion about the company policy regarding computer use?

    A. "I'll keep shopping anyway because I need to get a present for my sister's birthday."

    B. "Can you explain why the policy states that employees can't shop online?"

    C. "I can use my computer to send e-mails to co-workers."

    D. "When can I take my lunch break today?"

For more Chapter 3 assessment questions, please visit www.mysteckvaughn.com/WORK

Check your answers on page 166.

4 Cooperate with Others

Cooperation is a highly valued workplace skill that requires you to understand and respect the needs, ideas, and contributions of others. In this chapter, you will learn key skills and strategies that will strengthen your social skills and help you work as part of a team.

Key Skills for Cooperation in the Workplace

Essential Tasks

Interact with others
in ways that are friendly, courteous, and tactful and that demonstrate respect for others' ideas, opinions, and contributions

Offer clear input
on personal interests and attitudes so that others can understand one's actions and reactions and to clarify one's position

Build on What You Know

Have you ever ordered a large piece of furniture or sports equipment that had to be put together? Staring at a box full of parts and trying to make sense of the printed diagrams can be a daunting experience. It helps if someone else is there to help figure it out.

The same is true in the workplace. Since it is impossible to do everything on your own, you will need to **cooperate** with co-workers to achieve your goals. Working together can sometimes present challenges, such as the conflicts you learned about in Lessons 5 and 6. In these situations, you may need to make an extra effort to be cooperative. Think about the common goals you share, and remember that treating your co-workers with respect will go a long way toward creating a cooperative work environment.

In Real Life   Helping a New Co-Worker

Fred has been working at a lumber yard for several years. One afternoon, he is packing up to go home and notices that his new co-worker Jim is way behind on a special order. The customer will be picking up the order in the morning, and Jim is not even halfway through completing it. Fred asks if there is a problem, and Jim says that he is stressed out because he is running behind. Jim explains that this project is taking him extra time because he doesn't know where everything is, and he isn't familiar with some of the tools he needs to complete the job.

With a classmate, discuss the following questions. Share your ideas with the class.

1. Should Fred help the new co-worker? Why or why not?

2. Do Fred and Jim share a common goal?

3. How would you have felt if you were Jim?

4. What would you do if you were Fred?

Teacher Reminder
Review the teacher lesson at
www.mysteckvaughn.com/WORK

A Cooperative Workplace

In a cooperative workplace, co-workers demonstrate respect for each other and their customers. They communicate clearly and support each other to get the job done. Workplace conflicts are kept to a minimum. Doesn't that sound like the kind of place where you would like to work? You can help make it happen by being the kind of employee you would want to work with.

- **Be friendly.** A cooperative workplace depends on workers who are nice to one another and have a positive attitude.

- **Be courteous.** When you behave in a way that is polite and considerate, you create a feeling of respect and helpfulness in the workplace.

- **Be tactful.** Communicating clearly and trying to avoid upsetting others will reduce conflict in the workplace and help create a peaceful, productive work environment.

When co-workers demonstrate these qualities, they enjoy a respectful and cooperative workplace. Although some workplace conflicts may still occur, these behaviors can help resolve them and keep them from escalating.

Talk about the behaviors below. How does each one either help or hinder a cooperative work environment? Share your ideas with the class.

	Helpful	Not Helpful
Smiling and saying "Good morning" to a co-worker.		
Greeting customers when they walk into a store.		
Ignoring a co-worker's request for help.		
Offering to help a customer who looks lost.		
Interrupting a co-worker when he or she is speaking.		
Making fun of a co-worker's favorite hobby.		
Inviting a new co-worker to have lunch with you.		

Read the following questions. Discuss your answers with the class.

5. What are some ways that employees can be friendly? Why might that be important in the workplace?

6. When might it be difficult to be courteous?

7. How could being tactful help you resolve a workplace conflict?

> **Workplace Tip**
>
> To promote a respectful work environment:
>
> - Treat others as you would like to be treated.
> - Be considerate of others' ideas, opinions, and contributions.

Develop Your Skills

To create the best possible work environment, employees must have a cooperative attitude. They should try to be friendly, courteous, and tactful, even in difficult situations.

Be Friendly

Being friendly to co-workers does not mean that you have to be good friends with them. In any workplace, you may encounter people who have opinions, attitudes, or styles that conflict with yours. Even so, you can still greet your co-workers with a pleasant smile each morning and ask how they are doing. You can say positive things instead of complaining. It does not take a great deal of time or energy to be friendly. For instance, even if you are busy, you can offer a friendly response instead of an abrupt answer when someone asks you about your weekend.

> **Examples:**
> "My weekend was great, thanks. How was yours?" *friendly*
> "Fine. I hate Mondays." *unfriendly*

Be Courteous

Being **courteous** means being polite and considerate of others. Sometimes you can be courteous without saying a word by remaining calm and listening to someone. It is especially important to be courteous when you interact with customers. Following these three simple steps can help you to be courteous when you encounter an unhappy customer:

1. Allow the customer to explain the problem.

2. Put yourself in the customer's position.

3. Apologize for any inconvenience, and offer a solution.

Workplace Tip

When you are listening to a customer, remember to:
- Put yourself in the customer's shoes so you can understand why he or she is unhappy.
- Express your understanding of the customer's feelings.

Read the scenario and answer the questions that follow. Discuss your responses with a classmate.

One day, a customer drops off a prescription in the pharmacy where Mei works. Mei tells him that it should be ready in about 30 minutes. When the customer returns half an hour later, his prescription is not ready. Mei explains that the pharmacist has been very busy and assures the customer that his prescription will be ready in just a few minutes. She says that she is sorry for the wait and thanks the customer for his patience. The customer thanks Mei and takes a seat in the waiting area.

1. How was Mei courteous to the customer?

2. How did Mei's courteous behavior help the situation?

Be Tactful

Sometimes it's difficult to be friendly and courteous when you do not agree with a co-worker's opinion or a customer's complaint. Being **tactful** is a strategy that can help you manage your reactions in these difficult situations. When you are tactful, you make an effort to communicate in ways that are respectful of another person's feelings and point of view.

Being tactful does not mean simply telling the other person what he or she wants to hear. Instead, it means thinking about what you need to say and sharing the information in a way that is not hurtful or upsetting. To be tactful in a difficult workplace situation, always consider how you would like others to speak to you and remember the tips below. These tips can help you reduce conflicts and promote a pleasant work environment:

Do	Don't
Think before you speak.	Let your emotions take over.
Choose your words carefully.	Say whatever comes to mind.
Respect the person's point of view.	Attack the person's ideas.
Think of positive things to say.	Focus on the negatives.

Read the scenario. Then discuss the question that follows with a classmate.

Darryl has been a mechanic at Busy Auto for six months. He attends a meeting where his supervisor, Mr. Lopez, explains that business is down, and the company needs to reduce its costs. Mr. Lopez then outlines a new schedule with reduced hours for mechanics who have been with the company for less than a year.

Darryl is angry about the new schedule, and he thinks it is unfair to the newer mechanics. Also, he is worried because the new schedule means that he will earn less money, and he may be forced to find a second job. When Mr. Lopez asks if any employees have questions or concerns that they would like to discuss, Darryl raises his hand.

3. How can Darryl express his concerns tactfully?

GOT IT?	To help create a positive, respectful, and cooperative workplace:

- Be friendly to your co-workers and customers.

- Be courteous and treat others how you would like to be treated.

- Be tactful when you communicate your ideas and opinions.

To-Do List

Remember to follow these steps when applying your knowledge:

❏ **Be friendly**

❏ **Be courteous**

❏ **Be tactful**

Apply Your Knowledge

A cooperative workplace is one in which co-workers help one another and treat each other with respect.

As you read the following scenarios, think about the key skills for cooperation that you have learned in this lesson. Select what you think is the best response and the worst response to each situation.

1. Your co-worker Brian is going on vacation next week. Your supervisor asks you to complete Brian's tasks while he is away. The last time Brian went on vacation, he left you with disorganized folders, and you had to spend hours finding the documents you needed. What should you do?

   A. Meet with Brian before he goes on vacation to organize all of the documents that you may need.

   B. Spend extra time organizing Brian's folders while he is away on vacation.

   C. Ask your co-workers if they have ever covered for Brian and had the same problems.

   D. Refuse to cover for Brian and tell your supervisor that Brian is disorganized.

Best Answer		Worst Answer	

2. You work at a sporting goods store that has many different locations. Over the past month, the location where you work has been slower than some of the other stores. Your store manager explains that the company's new outlet store in a city nearby has been extremely busy. She asks you and a co-worker to transfer temporarily to the outlet store to help train new employees. You want to help, but working at the outlet store would add twenty minutes to your commute. The longer commute would cost you extra money in gas as well as day care expenses for your children. What should you do?

   A. Talk to your co-worker and complain about how unfair the manager's decision is.

   B. Tell your manager that you refuse to transfer to any other locations unless you get a raise.

   C. Explain to your manager that you would like to help, and work with her to find a solution.

   D. Ask to stay with a friend or family member who lives close to the outlet store.

Best Answer		Worst Answer	

3. You work at a bakery. A customer comes in to pick up a birthday cake that he ordered for his son. You locate the cake and show it to the customer. He opens the box and quickly slams it closed. Then he starts complaining that he ordered a vanilla cake with chocolate frosting, but this cake is chocolate with vanilla frosting. What should you do?

A. Tell the customer that the mix-up was probably his own fault.

B. Apologize for the error and prepare a new cake as quickly as possible.

C. Ask your manager to deal with the unhappy customer.

D. Explain that chocolate cake is better than the vanilla cake anyway.

Best Answer		Worst Answer	

In Real Life **Put Your Skills to Work!**

One of your co-workers wears a very strong perfume. You think you are allergic to the perfume because you start coughing and sneezing whenever you are near her. You also have overheard other co-workers complain about the perfume. You want to tell your co-worker, but you do not want to make her feel bad.

Think about the problem you are facing and put your skills to work! How will you approach your co-worker? What will you say?

Workplace Tip

Discussing a problem tactfully with a co-worker is challenging.
- Choose your words carefully.
- Say something positive.
- Being considerate of your co-worker's feelings.

Think About It!

What can you do to help create a respectful work environment?

How can the key skills for cooperation help you in workplace situations?

In a cooperative work environment, people are helpful and treat each other with respect. Conflicts are kept to a minimum. When conflicts do arise, they are resolved in constructive ways. Having a cooperative attitude can help create this kind of work environment. Being friendly, courteous, and tactful to your co-workers and customers will help you communicate effectively. Practice these key skills for cooperation to become the kind of co-worker that you would want to work with.

Answer Key

1. The best answer is A. Meeting with Brian before he goes on vacation is a cooperative way to prevent problems when you cover for him. The worst answer is D. Refusing to cover for a co-worker is not cooperative behavior.

2. The best answer is C. Working with your manager to find a solution is a cooperative response. The worst answer is B. Refusing to transfer unless you get a raise is not tactful.

3. The best answer is B. Apologizing and working to correct the error is a courteous way to address the customer's complaint. The worst answer is A. Blaming the customer for the error is not courteous.

Test Your WRC Skills

Select the best response and the worst response to each situation.

1. You are given blueprints and materials for a welding project. When you are looking over the measurements, you find that some materials were cut too short. You ask your foreman about the problem, and he explains that a new co-worker made the mistakes and cut the materials the wrong lengths. Your foreman asks you to redo the work and talk to your new co-worker about what he did wrong. How should you handle this situation?

Best	Worst	
○	○	As you redo the work, show the new co-worker how to measure correctly.
○	○	Tell your new co-worker to be careful when he is cutting materials.
○	○	Complain to your friends about the new co-worker's mistakes.
○	○	Tell the new co-worker that he messed up and he better not do it again.

2. The administrative assistant where you work is running late because his car broke down. He calls and tells you that yesterday he forgot to make copies of the agenda for this morning's staff meeting. He has already asked you to fill in for him several times this week. How should you handle this situation?

Best	Worst	
○	○	Call your supervisor and complain that the administrative assistant is not doing his job.
○	○	Calmly explain that you do not mind making the copies, but his requests this week have been excessive.
○	○	Tell the administrative assistant that he needs to get his act together and then hang up the phone.
○	○	Make extra copies of the agendas for all the meetings just in case the administrative assistant forgets.

3. At the end of a long shift at a grocery store, it is time to clock out. As you are walking toward the time clock, you pass a self-checkout lane and notice a customer having a problem paying for her groceries. You see the customer swipe her credit card, and the card reader keeps beeping and saying "Cannot read card." How should you handle this situation?

Best	Worst	
○	○	Tell the customer to pay with a different type of credit card.
○	○	Ignore the customer and clock out for the day.
○	○	Ask other cashiers if their card readers have been having problems.
○	○	Tell the customer that you will go get a supervisor who can help her.

4. You are close friends with a co-worker who recently had a baby. This co-worker has been sending you e-mails containing attachments with videos and pictures of her new baby. You enjoy hearing about the baby, but you find these e-mails distracting at work, and receiving her attachments sometimes causes your computer to freeze. How should you handle this situation?

Best	Worst	
○	○	Call the IT department and ask why the computer is freezing.
○	○	Ask your co-worker to send all personal e-mails to your home computer.
○	○	Install a program to filter attachments received on your work computer.
○	○	Ask your co-worker to keep the news about her baby to herself.

5. Kyle has been in meetings all morning. At noon, he finally gets a twenty-minute break before he has to leave work to meet a client at a job site. As he is rushing to the break room to grab his lunch, a new co-worker stops him and explains that she can't get her new voicemail to work. She asks Kyle for help, but he has no time. How should Kyle handle this situation?

Best	Worst	
○	○	Help the new co-worker set up her voicemail and go to the job site late.
○	○	Wave his hands to indicate that he is in a rush and can't stop to help.
○	○	Offer to help the co-worker when he returns from the job site.
○	○	Ask other co-workers if they are having problems with their voicemails.

6. Holly and Diego work at a factory. They are the first two workers on a complex assembly line. Holly's job is to arrange materials in their proper places and send them to Diego's station. Then Diego bolts these parts together and sends them to the next part of the line. Lately, Holly has been arranging the materials so slowly that Diego cannot put many parts together. Workers at the end of the line are complaining to Diego about the delay. How should Diego handle this situation?

Best	Worst	
○	○	Yell at Holly to speed things up because her work is slowing down the entire assembly line.
○	○	Tell the workers at the end of the assembly line to be more patient while they wait.
○	○	Ask other workers on the assembly line if they think that the factory should hire more employees.
○	○	Go talk to Holly to ask if there is a problem, and see if she needs help with something.

Check your answers on page 167.

Essential Tasks

Recognize and respond to social cues (e.g., speaker's need for validation, speaker's comprehension checks, opportunities to take the floor, end of conversation) in conversation

Workplace Tip

When you listen in the workplace:

- Wait patiently for the speaker to finish his or her thoughts.
- Focus on what the speaker is saying, not on what you want to say next.
- Identify key phrases that tell you when and how to respond.

Develop Your Skills **Answer Key**

1. The customer needs help printing in color.

2. *What do you think?*

3. Possible answer: "I'm so glad to hear that you like your printer. Sorry it's giving you a little trouble today. You may be right about that ink cartridge. Let's find out. What are the model numbers of your printer and the ink cartridges?"

Active Listening

Build on What You Know

Have you ever talked to someone who always interrupts before you can finish? Or maybe the person doesn't answer your question or changes the subject unexpectedly. Talking with someone who does not recognize social cues can be a frustrating experience.

You know that giving clear and tactful input to your co-workers and customers is a key to building a cooperative workplace. Similarly, knowing how to listen actively and courteously to the input of others will also help you cooperate in your workplace.

Develop Your Skills

Listening for social cues will help you understand how and when to respond to a speaker. The following phrases, and many others like them, perform certain functions in a conversation. Listening for these social cues will help you understand the speaker and respond appropriately:

Phrase	Function
"I'm glad you asked."	Acknowledges a question
"Does that sound right to you?"	Asks for validation or support
"Do you have any questions?" "Do you have anything to add?"	Gives listeners the opportunity to respond
"Thank you for your time."	Ends the conversation

Role-play the following situation with a fellow classmate. Remember to listen carefully for clues that will help you determine how and when to respond to the speaker. Complete your role-play by discussing the questions that follow.

You are a customer service representative for a printer company. A customer calls and says: *I love my TSX printer. I bought one last month and haven't had any problems until today. I need to print a chart in color for a work project, but I can only get the printer to print in black and white. I have tried restarting my computer and checking the printer settings. I think there may be a problem with one of the ink cartridges. What do you think?*

1. What does the speaker want or need?

2. Which phrase indicates your opportunity to respond?

3. What would be an appropriate response to the customer?

Apply Your Knowledge

Read the following scenario and answer the questions.

Your supervisor calls you into her office. She says: *Thank you so much for helping Luis and Sylvia feel welcome. I notice that whenever I hire new members of our team, you are the first person to greet them and help them adjust. Because you are so friendly and welcoming, I would like to offer you the opportunity to lead our new employee orientations. I think it would be a great way for you to develop your leadership skills. I realize that it will be a challenge to fit this added responsibility into your busy schedule, but I think it is a position that you will enjoy and thrive in. Does this sound like something that you would like to do?*

4. Which phrase tells you why you are being offered the position?

5. What words or phrases indicate the possible negative aspects of this opportunity?

6. What would be an appropriate response if you were not sure that you wanted to accept the position?

Test Your WRC Skills Scenario 12

Listen to hear a presentation at a safety meeting. You may listen to the presentation more than once before answering the question.

Active Listening Scenarios are available at **www.mysteckvaughn.com/WORK**.

Which of the following statements could likely take place NEXT?

A. "If there are no further questions, let's break for lunch."

B. "Don't forget to read the hazardous waste section of your safety manual."

C. "Does anyone have any questions about the handout?"

D. "I look forward to seeing you at the job site next week."

Check your answer on page 167.

To-Do List

Remember to follow these steps when applying your knowledge:

❑ **Wait for the speaker to finish**

❑ **Listen for social cues**

❑ **Respond appropriately**

Apply Your Knowledge **Answer Key**

4. *Because you are so friendly and welcoming*

5. *Challenge, added responsibility, busy schedule*

6. Possible answer: "Thank you. I am honored that you thought of me for this opportunity. The position sounds really interesting, but I agree that it might pose a challenge. I wouldn't want my other work to suffer. Do you mind if I take a little time to think about it and get back to you tomorrow?"

Work as Part of a Team—Personal

Build on What You Know

When you were a kid, did you ever pick players for a sports team? Why did you choose certain kids over others? Was it because they played well and had a good attitude? Or was it because they hogged the ball and put down their teammates? You probably chose players you knew would help your team win the game and who would make playing an enjoyable experience. In other words, you selected kids who were **team players**.

Just as in sports, team players in the workplace contribute to a common goal and make working together a pleasant experience. Managers look for team players when they make their hiring decisions because the success of their business depends on people who can work well together. For example, workers may need to collaborate to complete a project or to make sure a customer gets what he or she needs. Being a team player in the workplace means demonstrating that you have the qualities it takes to help you and others succeed.

In Real Life   Team Talk

Jayden's interview for a wait staff position at a new restaurant is going extremely well. The manager, Helena, is impressed with Jayden's application. To make sure that he will work well with the rest of the staff, Helena says: *Tell me about your ability to work as part of a team.*

Jayden decides to respond by sharing a recent volunteer experience. He explains: *I learned a lot about teamwork when I helped build houses for families in need. Each volunteer had a different task, but we all worked toward the same goal. I was in charge of getting everybody the supplies they needed. The other volunteers counted on me to do my part so that they could do theirs. We also had to communicate well to solve problems and to help each other. Together, we were able to successfully build several houses.*

Discuss the following questions. Share your ideas with the class.

1. How does Jayden show that he is a team player?

2. In what ways is a restaurant staff a team?

3. Why is it important that Jayden work well with the restaurant staff?

The Perfect Teammate

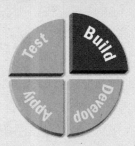

You learned all about cooperation in Lesson 7. Recall that cooperation means working with others to achieve a common goal. Team players know how to be friendly, courteous, and tactful. They are able to work with all kinds of people to complete group tasks.

There are many qualities team players possess in addition to the ability to cooperate. In order to think about what makes a good team player, identify the qualities you would want in a teammate at work.

Imagine you could create the perfect teammate. What qualities would this person have? Place a check mark next to the qualities that you would like your teammate to possess. Then answer the questions below.

❏ Good listener	❏ Self-absorbed
❏ Irresponsible	❏ Stubborn
❏ Cooperative	❏ Communicative
❏ Helpful	❏ Mean
❏ Neglectful	❏ Honest
❏ Trustworthy	❏ Incapable
❏ Rude	❏ Respectful
❏ Committed	❏ Flexible
❏ Skilled	❏ Polite
❏ Dishonest	❏ Supportive
❏ Lazy	❏ Insincere

4. What do you think are the top three qualities that make a good teammate? What are the top three qualities that make a bad teammate?

5. Do you think it is important for a team player to have only a few of the qualities you selected? Why or why not?

6. Which of the above qualities do you possess that make you a team player?

7. Which qualities could you focus on improving to make yourself a better team player?

Develop Your Skills

An important part of being a team player is developing and keeping good relationships with co-workers, supervisors, clients, and customers. In order to do this, you must be able to adjust your actions to account for the needs of others and the tasks to be accomplished. This is not hard to do if you use the following guidelines.

Be Flexible

Being flexible means being able to adapt to new situations and ideas. Team players don't become stressed or angry when new approaches are tried or problems occur. They keep a positive attitude and adjust their actions to achieve group goals.

In addition, team players are open to different ways of doing things. They see the benefit of acknowledging other viewpoints and strategies. They can compromise because they recognize what is best for the team. Team players are not stubborn or selfish, but are accommodating and easy-going. They listen well and incorporate the feedback of other co-workers.

Sometimes it can be hard to be flexible—especially if you believe that your way of doing something is the best. Use these tips to help you be more open-minded and flexible in the workplace:

- Remember that there is usually not one "right" way to do something.
- Keep in mind that some things are not worth fighting over. Choose your battles. If it doesn't impact the ultimate goal, let it go.
- Listen to the reasons why others feel or act the way they do.
- Realize that you'll be less stressed if you can "go with the flow."

 Discuss with a classmate why the following statements are inflexible.

1. I always use a binder to file my client's orders, so you should too.

2. My manager asked me to help her with an extra task, but that's not part of my job description.

Be Proactive

Employees who are **proactive** identify what needs to be done—and do it. They are not **passive**. If they discover a problem, they seek a solution. If they need help, they ask for assistance. If someone else needs help, they offer it. Proactive employees are team players because they participate actively as part of the group.

> ### Workplace Tip
> Being proactive does not mean asking for lots of extra work to show that you are a good employee. It simply means taking responsibility and the necessary actions to make sure you and others succeed.

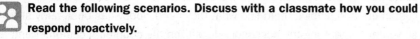

Example:

Sheila is having trouble faxing a document to a client, and you pretend not to notice because you have work to do. *passive*

Sheila is having trouble faxing a document to a client, so you take a few minutes to explain to her how to use the fax machine. *proactive*

A big part of being proactive is practicing good communication. Sharing ideas and information, as well as expressing your own needs, shows that you are involved and committed to the team's success.

Read the following scenarios. Discuss with a classmate how you could respond proactively.

3. You are asked to clean the cafeteria floor but don't understand how to use a floor buffer.

4. You notice that a co-worker accidentally forgot to flip the store sign from "Closed" to "Open."

Be Dependable

Team players are always dependable. They do what they are assigned and complete their tasks on time. Others can always rely on them to work hard and take on a fair share of the workload.

Being dependable is important because teams often divide tasks among their members. If one person does not do his or her part, it can affect the ability of the rest of the team to do their parts.

Read the following scenario and then answer the questions below.

Claire, Mitch, and Naveen work at an automotive manufacturing plant. Claire is responsible for transporting car parts, such as brake rotors, from the supplier to the plant. Mitch works on the production assembly line, installing brake systems. Naveen inspects the brake systems on the finished cars.

5. What would happen if Claire didn't do her job? Mitch? Naveen?

6. Why is it important that Claire, Mitch, and Naveen are dependable?

> **GOT IT?** Being a team player will help you get the job you want and build a successful career. To be a team player:
>
> - Be flexible by adapting to new situations, ideas, and ways of doing things.
> - Be proactive by figuring out what needs to be done and doing it.
> - Be dependable by completing your assignments thoroughly and on time.

Answer Key

1. The statement is inflexible because it allows for only one way to file the orders.

2. The statement is inflexible because you are not willing to accommodate your manager's request.

3. Ask a co-worker or supervisor how to use the floor buffer.

4. Flip the sign to "Open" yourself.

5. If Claire didn't do her job, Mitch would not have the parts he needs to assemble the brake systems. If Mitch didn't do his job, Naveen would have nothing to inspect. If Naveen didn't do her job, the car would be dangerous to drive and customers would be put at risk.

6. Each worker needs to be dependable for the team to accomplish the overall goal of manufacturing cars.

Apply Your Knowledge

Being a team player can help you manage a variety of workplace situations. Remember to think about the needs of others and adjust your actions as needed to accomplish the goals of the team.

As you read the following scenarios, think about the qualities of a team player. Select what you think is the best response and the worst response to each situation.

1. You work at a small clothing store. Your primary responsibility is to ring up customers at the register. Margery, a co-worker, is in charge of welcoming customers and helping them find what they need. Today has been fairly slow, so you are organizing the accessory display on the counter. A customer enters the store and seems to be looking for something in particular. Margery is busy helping another customer. What should you do?

   A. Wait for Margery to help the new customer since that is her responsibility.

   B. Ask the customer if you can help her find something.

   C. Hope that the customer finds what she needs so that you can ring her up at the register.

   D. Yell out to Margery across the store to let her know that she needs to help another customer.

Best Answer		Worst Answer	

2. The tile company that you work for has been installing tile in several rooms of a new house. You are finally ready to install the tile in the upstairs bathroom. Eli, your co-worker, was supposed to have the tiles cut and ready for you to put in, but you find that he has fallen behind on this task because he had to fix a problem with the tile saw. What should you do?

   A. Help Eli by measuring and marking the tiles that need to be cut.

   B. Take your lunch break while Eli finishes cutting the tile.

   C. Tell your supervisor that Eli is making you fall behind.

   D. Tell Eli that he needs to work faster to make up time.

Best Answer		Worst Answer	

You work as a ticket agent for an airline. The stormy weather in your city has caused all the outgoing flights to be delayed or canceled. You are expecting a long line of frustrated travelers to form in front of the ticket counter. In addition to re-scheduling flights, you will need to make hotel arrangements for the travelers from out of town. Only two other agents are working behind the counter with you.

Think about the problem you are facing and put your skills to work! How can you work with the other ticket agents to meet the goal of assisting all the travelers? How can you show that you are a team player?

Workplace Tip

When deciding how to best meet your goal, think about:

- How to adapt to this new situation.
- Ways to be proactive that will ease the stress of travelers and co-workers.
- How to show that you are a dependable worker.

Think About It!

What kinds of teams will you encounter in your workplace?

How can you be a better team player?

You will come across many different kinds of teams in the workplace. You might be part of a large company "team" and part of a smaller project team within the company. You might work as a team with a customer or group of clients. The team might be called a "team," or it might just be a group of people who work together to reach a common goal. No matter what kind of team you are on, it is important to be a team player. This is not hard to do if you practice being the kind of person you would want to work with.

Answer Key

1. The best answer is B. Since you are not busy and Margery is, you should be proactive by providing help when needed. The worst answer is D. Yelling at Margery is a disrespectful way to tell her to do something she is clearly too busy to do. This behavior is also likely to make the customers feel uncomfortable.

2. The best answer is A. Offering assistance will help you and Eli accomplish the ultimate goal of installing the bathroom tiles. The worst answer is C. Your supervisor will probably tell you to help Eli and wonder why you did not think of that on your own.

Test Your WRC Skills

Select the best response and the worst response to each situation.

1. The morning rush at the coffee shop where you work has finally ended. Now the store is getting just a few customers every hour. How should you handle this situation?

Best	Worst	
○	○	Take a long break because there is nothing to do.
○	○	Wait patiently until the manager gives you a task.
○	○	Begin clearing the tables and preparing for the midday rush.
○	○	Look busy even though you don't know what you should be doing.

2. You inspect and clean vehicles for a car rental company. You have been asked to prepare a red sports car for an afternoon pick-up. How should you handle this situation?

Best	Worst	
○	○	Wait until fifteen minutes before the customer is expected to arrive before getting the car ready.
○	○	Thoroughly prepare the car well before the customer arrives.
○	○	Decide not to prepare the car because there are other cars in the lot that the customer could rent.
○	○	Clean and inspect the car quickly so that that you can leave for lunch.

3. You work as a front desk clerk for a hotel. When you try to confirm the room reservation for a family that has just arrived, you find that another clerk accidentally canceled the reservation. How should you handle this situation?

Best	Worst	
○	○	Tell the family that your co-worker is always messing up, and now there's nothing you can do to help them.
○	○	Assign the family a room, even though it doesn't compare to the room they had reserved.
○	○	Get your co-worker to resolve the problem, since she was the one who created the problem in the first place.
○	○	Apologize for the error and work with the family to find a suitable, available room.

4. Your supervisor has asked you to prune and trim all the trees in a large apartment complex. As you are working, another member of your crew seems annoyed because she needs to use the shears to complete a quick task. How should you handle this situation?

Best	Worst	
○	○	Explain that she can have the shears when you finish with them.
○	○	Offer to stop for a few minutes so that she can complete her task.
○	○	Tell her to wait until tomorrow since your job is more important.
○	○	Tell her that you will take care of her task when you finish your own.

5. The construction company you work for is putting a new roof on a house. Modesto, another worker, has placed the ladder against the house and is getting ready to climb up. You know that somebody should be holding the ladder at the bottom to steady it. How should you handle this situation?

Best	Worst	
○	○	Walk over to the ladder and steady it yourself.
○	○	Ask another worker to hold the ladder for Modesto.
○	○	Don't do anything and hope that Modesto doesn't hurt himself.
○	○	Tell Modesto not to climb the ladder.

6. You have just started working as a receptionist at a doctor's office. You need to transfer a phone call to an outside line but don't know how to do this. How should you handle this situation?

Best	Worst	
○	○	Tell the patient on the phone that she will have to call back when the other receptionist is working.
○	○	Press the button that you believe will transfer the call and hope for the best.
○	○	Place the patient on hold and quickly ask a co-worker to show you how to transfer the call.
○	○	Place the patient on hold while you try to locate the phone manual in the storage room.

Check your answers on page 168.

Active Listening

Build on What You Know

Have you ever misunderstood what someone has told you? Maybe you weren't listening carefully enough, or maybe the person's explanation was unclear. What were the consequences of the misunderstanding? Were you embarrassed? Perhaps you failed to complete an important task as a result. How did your mistake affect others?

When you work as part of a team, it is important to understand what your teammates tell you, even if it does not seem to affect you at the time. Practice being a proactive team player by confirming your understanding of what you hear and asking for clarification when needed.

Develop Your Skills

Here are some ways to be sure you understand what you hear:

- **Paraphrase and restate.** Use your own words to repeat back to the speaker what you heard. If necessary, include key words or phrases from what the speaker said to show that you understand.

- **Summarize.** If you are given a lot of information, identify the main points. Write them down so you remember them. Repeat your summary to the speaker so he or she can correct any misunderstandings.

- **Ask questions.** Clear up any confusion by asking the speaker or another listener to clarify what was said.

Role-play the following situation with a classmate. Complete your role- play by discussing the following questions.

Customer: *I'm having a problem with this MP3 player. I can't get it to import music from my computer. I tried to find a solution in the manual, but it was very frustrating.*

Store Employee: *That does sound frustrating. Maybe I can help. You said you can't get the player to import music from your computer. Can you explain the steps you followed so I can understand the problem better?*

1. What words or phrases does the store employee restate in her response?

2. How does the store employee make sure that she understands what is wrong with the MP3 player?

Apply Your Knowledge

Read the following scenario and answer the questions.

The superintendent has called a meeting with your construction crew to review an important safety rule: *I would like to remind all of you to follow our company's safety policies. Specifically, please remember to wear hard hats at all times while at the job site. It has come to my attention that this policy has not been taken very seriously lately. We work in dangerous conditions and must do all we can to prevent injuries. If you see another worker without a hard hat, please remind him or her to put it on. It is everybody's responsibility to look out for themselves and the people around them. Does anyone have any questions?*

3. Paraphrase and restate what you should do if another worker is not wearing a hard hat.

4. What are the main points from the meeting? How can you remember them?

5. How could you confirm your understanding of which locations are considered part of the job site?

Test Your WRC Skills Scenario 13

Listen to hear part of a meeting regarding an upcoming conference. You may listen to the meeting more than once before answering the question.

Active Listening Scenarios are available at www.mysteckvaughn.com/WORK.

Which of the following would a member of the cleaning crew MOST likely say to show an understanding of his assignment?

A. "The storage room was just cleaned out last month."

B. "Floor buffers can actually be quite difficult to operate."

C. "I have never set up a sound system before, but I will try."

D. "I'll buff the floors while Sylvia cleans the tables and chairs."

Check your answer on page 168.

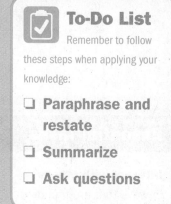

To-Do List
Remember to follow these steps when applying your knowledge:

❏ **Paraphrase and restate**

❏ **Summarize**

❏ **Ask questions**

Apply Your Knowledge **Answer Key**

3. Tell workers who are not wearing hard hats to put them on.

4. Wear hard hats at all times while at a site and look out for yourself and others. Write down the main points to remember them.

5. Ask the speaker or another listener for clarification.

Work as Part of a Team— Interpersonal

Essential Tasks

Interact with others in ways that are friendly, courteous, and tactful and that demonstrate respect for others' ideas, opinions, and contributions

Use strategies to seek input from others in order to understand their actions and reactions

Build on What You Know

Have you ever been a part of a team? You may have played sports in school and been a part of that team. However, there are many other different types of teams. You may be a member of a family team, a community team, a school team, a social committee team, or even a work team. Remember, there is no "I" in the word *team*. To work effectively as part of a team, you need to have **interpersonal skills**; these are often called *people skills*.

In Real Life   How Good Is the Team?

Jared has just been hired as a cashier at a local interior design store. He has some creative ideas on how to improve the company's image with customers. At a team meeting, Jared tries to explain his ideas, but he is nervous and none of his words come out right. In fact, some team members laugh at his inability to speak clearly. Jared is very embarrassed at not being able to effectively communicate his ideas. After the meeting, Teva, one of the team's members, talks with Jared. She tells him that it sounds like he has some great ideas. She suggests that he first develop a presentation that accurately reflects his ideas and then present it at the next meeting.

Jared takes Teva's suggestion. He creates a presentation, and practices until he is comfortable. At the next meeting, Jared is able to present his ideas clearly to the group. The group discusses each of his ideas. Even though the company decides not to implement all of Jared's ideas, he feels like he is an important part of the team.

 Discuss the following questions. Share your ideas with the class.

1. How would you have felt if you were Jared?

2. How would you have handled this situation?

3. What part did Teva play in creating a team attitude for everyone?

4. What could have been the result if Teva had not spoken with Jared?

Teacher Reminder
Review the teacher lesson at
www.mysteckvaughn.com/WORK

112 Situational Judgment and Active Listening

Your Teamwork Experience

How do you become more effective at working with others? First, think about the last time you worked with a team. Remember who was on the team, the team's purpose, and the role of each team member.

 Fill in the following chart. Discuss your results with the class.

Question	Often	Sometimes	Never
1. I felt comfortable working as part of a team.			
2. Everyone on our team respected and supported each other.			
3. I felt my contributions were valued by the rest of the team.			
4. No one person dominated the team. Everyone had a chance to speak.			
5. I was able to share my ideas and opinions.			
6. Our team stayed on the tasks we were assigned and didn't waste time.			
7. I was actively involved in completing the task successfully.			
8. We took turns taking different roles on the team.			
9. I had the opportunity to lead the discussion.			

No matter what role you play on a team or what tasks you are assigned, there is always room for personal improvement.

Ask yourself the following questions. Discuss your answers with the class.

5. What are three skills you possess that make you a valuable team member?

6. What are three interpersonal skills that you would like to improve? Write these three skills on an index card. Make it a goal to practice these skills each day.

> **Workplace Tip**
>
> Communicating effectively, being on time, being positive, having great ideas, and having a good sense of humor are examples of effective interpersonal skills.

Develop Your Skills

Getting along with others in the workplace is a talent that requires interpersonal skills. Practice the following skills at home and in the workplace. See if they make an impact!

Using Self-Talk to Create a Positive Message

Employers want staff members who have positive attitudes. It's important for you to be able to turn negative experiences at the workplace into an opportunity to do something positive. This can be difficult to do, especially when you are faced with a challenging task.

All of us have silent conversations in our heads known as **self-talk.** Self-talk consists of two inner voices, a **"positive" voice** and a **"negative" voice.** One way to change your attitude at work is to replace negative messages that you have with more positive ones.

> **Example:**
>
> "We'll never get this truck loaded." *negative message*
>
> "If we ask Tam to help us, we can get this truck loaded quickly." *positive message*

Change the following negative messages into more positive ones.

1. I am so much slower than everyone else. I knew I couldn't do the job right.

2. I know that I won't be able to get this financial report done today.

Dealing with Resistance

Everyone faces disagreements or **resistance** in life. However, sometimes a very minor disagreement can become worse and can cause problems at the workplace. How do you deal with a disagreement or an argument? The first thing to do is find out what the other person wants without losing sight of your own personal goals.

"I" messages are a good way to keep the argument from getting worse and making others feel defensive. Tell the other person how her or his behavior affects you by using the words "I," "me," or "my." By avoiding the use of the word "you," the other person may feel less defensive.

Example:

"You make me very angry when you talk on the phone during staff meetings." *negative*

"When you talk on the phone during staff meetings, I have a difficult time hearing our co-workers." *more positive*

Role-play the following scenarios with another student or friend. Practice using "I" messages when responding. You may wish to first write your "I" message before you practice saying it.

3. You are trying to complete a report, and a fellow worker is playing loud music on his computer.

4. You work as a ticket agent at a train station. A passenger is very angry because she has missed her train. She pushes ahead of everyone and begins to yell at you.

Applying Reflective Listening

It's important to understand what a person means when communicating. Have you ever heard the phrase "lost in translation"? Sometimes people get misunderstood; what they actually are trying to say isn't the message the listener understands. To make sure that you have understood what a person said, restate the message and then ask if you heard it correctly.

Example:

"I heard you say that it would be best if the company would purchase additional stock. Is that what you think needs to be done?"

Have a conversation with another classmate. Listen carefully and practice rephrasing what the person said and ask if you heard the message correctly.

GOT IT? **Successful interpersonal communication depends on you! When you speak:**

- Think carefully about what you say before you say it.
- Employ positive messages whenever possible.
- Use "I" messages when faced with co-workers' different viewpoints.
- Restate what a co-worker has said to better understand the person's intended message.

To-Do List

Remember to follow these steps when applying your knowledge:

❑ **Positive attitude**

❑ **"I" message**

❑ **Paraphrase**

Apply Your Knowledge

Solving situational judgment problems requires that you apply different types of skills in work-related situations.

As you read the following scenarios, think about the different types of interpersonal skills that you have learned in this lesson. Select what you think is the best response and the worst response to the situation.

1. You work at a factory. Your supervisor calls you on your day off and asks if you can cover your co-worker Damian's shift because he has called in sick. You have covered for Damian many times in the past six months, and you already have plans to go to the amusement park. Apologizing to your supervisor, you say that you cannot come in to work the extra shift because you have other plans. While waiting in line at the park, you see Damian ahead of you. What should you do?

    A. Do nothing because Damian's behavior is not your problem.

    B. Call your supervisor, tell her that Damian skipped work, and say that she should fire him immediately.

    C. Talk to Damian about his irresponsible behavior and tell him that if this happens again, you will need to tell your supervisor.

    D. Complain to your co-workers that Damian calls in sick too often.

Best Answer		Worst Answer	

2. You work as a cashier at the local bank. A new cashier, Beatrice, has just been hired. You notice that she is very nervous about completing the different types of tasks. You have been working at the bank for years and understand these tasks. You are often viewed as the team leader in the department because of your expertise. At the end of the workday, you notice that Beatrice is making a mistake when she closes out her register. What should you do?

    A. Let Beatrice make mistakes so that she gets fired from the position.

    B. Tell one of your co-workers to help Beatrice close out her register and complete her daily tasks.

    C. Call your supervisor and explain Beatrice's mistake.

    D. Show Beatrice how to avoid making mistakes and support her efforts as a new employee.

Best Answer		Worst Answer	

Put Your Skills to Work!

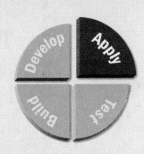

You are part of a team that has taken on a new project. As part of the project, you are meeting with four other members of the team. You are excited about the project and have worked hard to develop an initial plan. At the meeting, you begin to share your ideas with the group. Before you can finish explaining your plan, a team member interrupts and begins to say why it will not work. You try to respond, but the other team member continues to interrupt you. You feel strongly that your ideas are beneficial to the project, and you are frustrated that this team member always dominates the conversation whenever you are in a meeting.

Think about the problem you are facing and put your skills to work! How would you deal with the resistance and negative attitude of this co-worker? What skills will you use?

Workplace Tip

When making your decision, did you think about:

- How to stay positive?
- Using "I" messages?
- Understanding the team member's concerns?
- Rephrasing the team member's concerns?

Think About It!

What interpersonal skills do you need to practice the most?

How will you practice these skills?

The best way to practice is with a friend who will understand if the interaction doesn't go as well as you would like. Practicing new skills works best when you have the eyes and ears of others who can help you understand what you are doing well and spot areas where you can improve. Think of practicing with a friend as a rehearsal for a workplace scenario. Explain what you want to improve and ask your friend for feedback afterwards.

Answer Key

1. The best answer is C. Making a co-worker aware that his actions are wrong and letting him explain is the best course of action. The worst answer is B. Telling on a fellow worker can result in others not wanting you as part of the team.

2. The best answer is D. Working as a team is an important skill. Helping a new employee to do his or her job correctly is important to both the person and the company. The worst answer is A. Not working as a team creates a poor workplace environment. Helping others is important to the success of a business.

Test Your WRC Skills

Select the best response and the worst response to each situation.

1. You are a ticket agent for an airline. You have been on the job for four weeks. Today a passenger is very unhappy. He wants you to get him on an earlier flight, but the flight is full. The passenger becomes very angry and begins to shout at you. How should you handle this situation?

Best	Worst	
○	○	Shout back at the customer.
○	○	Leave your station.
○	○	Request a supervisor.
○	○	Quit your job.

2. You are one of ten employees who work in your office. Last week, everyone else received a new computer and printer, but you did not. How should you handle this situation?

Best	Worst	
○	○	Talk to your supervisor to see if a mistake was made.
○	○	Complain to your co-workers that it is unfair.
○	○	Confront your supervisor and demand a new computer.
○	○	Take a co-worker's computer and printer.

3. You are responsible for training all new clerks at a supermarket chain. You have been working with the new hires on how to close out a cash register at the end of the day. One of the new employees, Sarah, appears overwhelmed and goes into the restroom in tears. How should you handle this situation?

Best	Worst	
○	○	Send someone into the restroom so Sarah has somebody to talk with.
○	○	Continue the training with the rest of the employees and fill Sarah in later.
○	○	Contact Sarah's supervisor to discuss her behavior during training.
○	○	Talk with Sarah when she is calm, and ask her if something was said that upset her.

4. You just started working as a nursing assistant yesterday. This is your first full-time job. You wanted the job and want to do well, but your supervisor, Ms. Donato, intimidates you. Yesterday she told you, "You are making the beds all wrong! Don't make the beds like that!" Later, she came back, handed you a clipboard and said, "Here, fill in this chart." You didn't know how to fill in the chart. You are afraid that Ms. Donato will think that you aren't a good worker if you ask questions. How should you handle this situation?

Best	Worst	
○	○	Tell Ms. Donato that you want to do well, and ask her to explain things more clearly while you are still learning.
○	○	Watch how other employees complete the job and try to do better.
○	○	Explain your problem to a co-worker and ask what to do.
○	○	Complain about how unfair and incompetent Ms. Donato is as a supervisor.

5. You work for an insurance company. Each week the sales team meets to discuss new products and sales strategies. During today's meeting, Veronica is talking loudly on the telephone while the rest of the team is trying to solve a problem with one of the new products. You are having a difficult time listening to the conversation. How should you handle this situation?

Best	Worst	
○	○	Ask the supervisor to request that Veronica leave the meeting.
○	○	Tell Veronica that she is being her typical rude and loud self, just like everyone says.
○	○	Try to listen more closely and hope that you can hear most of the conversation.
○	○	Tell Veronica that because of her talking on the phone, you are having difficulty hearing what the supervisor is saying.

6. At your weekly staff meetings, one of your co-workers frequently interrupts the discussion to talk about the new house that she is building. Her constant interruptions make the meetings run late. How should you handle this situation?

Best	Worst	
○	○	Report your co-worker's behavior to your supervisor so that you have the information on the record.
○	○	Talk with your co-worker and request that she not discuss personal matters during the meeting, as it is disruptive.
○	○	Confront your co-worker during the meeting and loudly inform her that no one cares about her or her personal business.
○	○	Ignore your co-worker and try to schedule meetings when she is not available.

Check your answers on page 169.

Essential Tasks

Determine information and ideas relevant to purpose

Reconsider purpose based on new information

Workplace Tip

Pay attention only to the information that is relevant to the purpose of the communication. This helps you to focus on specific items and reduces the amount of information you have to process.

***Develop Your Skills* Answer Key**

1. Possible answer: "It sounds as if you are really upset about not receiving the sales price on your suit. I am sure that we can provide you with a satisfactory refund."

2. Not getting the sale price

3. Sometimes when people are angry they say things that they don't mean before they get to the real problem.

Active Listening

Build on What You Know

Have you ever been misunderstood or not taken seriously? How did you feel? What did you do to get your point across?

An important part of active listening is creating a connection and determining what the other person wants.

When you connect with someone, you are reacting to a problem or to good news as though it's part of your life. Being able to identify what is important to the person with whom you are speaking will assist you in becoming a more effective listener.

Develop Your Skills

How do you connect to the speaker? To establish a connection, you should:

- **Listen** for the main idea of the conversation.
- **Identify** information relevant to the purpose.
- **Link** what you are hearing to what you already know.
- **Check** for understanding.
- **Respond** to the information.

Role-play the following situation with a fellow classmate. Remember to connect to the speaker and follow the steps for identifying the relevant information before you respond. Complete your role-play by discussing the following questions.

A customer barges into your store. She is clearly upset about something. She says: *This is the worst store in town. You are always so expensive! I don't even know why I ever shop here. I am never going to come into your store again. The last time I was here I bought a new suit. It was supposed to be on sale, but when I got home I found that I had been charged the full price!*

1. What was your response to the customer?

2. What information was relevant to your response?

3. Why did the customer talk about other things not related to her problem?

Apply Your Knowledge

Read the following scenario and answer the questions.

You are a waiter at a restaurant. You supervisor has called a meeting to discuss recent absenteeism at the restaurant. At the meeting, your supervisor says: *Absenteeism is causing us problems in serving our customers. We don't have a full staff right now because no one wants to work the weekend evening shifts. I am really tired of having customers complain because they don't receive good service. In fact, just the other day I was at another restaurant with great service, and the food was excellent. I'd like for some of you to go there and see what you think. Maybe we could add some of the dishes to our menu. It's important for me to have team feedback, so what do each of you think?*

4. What was the purpose of the meeting?

5. What information is relevant to the purpose?

6. What information do you know?

7. What is the problem?

8. How would you respond?

Test Your WRC Skills Scenario 14

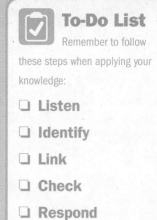

Listen to hear a conversation between two co-workers. You may listen to the conversation more than once before answering the question.

Active Listening scenarios available at www.mysteckvaughn.com/WORK.

Based on the conversation, what would be the best response for Karl to make next?

A. "Lena, I think it would be best if you didn't come to the next meeting until you are not so angry with Mabel."

B. "Lena, I am going to have to talk to the boss about how you feel about Mabel."

C. "Lena, your bonus idea may be just what is needed to boost our customer service."

D. "Lena, are you sure that there is enough money to provide bonuses this quarter?"

Check your answer on page 169.

Apply Your Knowledge **Answer Key**

4. To address the problem of absenteeism (Listen)

5. Not having a full staff, customers complaining (Identify)

6. If you don't have enough people working, customers won't get enough attention. (Link)

7. The restaurant needs to figure out how to get everybody to show up for their shifts. (Check)

8. Possible answer: "What about offering some kind of incentive or prize for working weekend evening shifts?" (Respond)

Skills for the Workplace

Social Skills

Your **social skills** are the skills you use to get along with people, both in the workplace and in your everyday life. People with well-developed social skills are pleasant to deal with. They get along easily with people and tend to do better in job interviews. Managers, co-workers, and customers perceive them as more skilled and capable than other co-workers with poor social skills. Fair or not, improving your social skills in the workplace has the potential to dramatically help your career. Consider the following key social skills for the workplace:

- **Exchange friendly greetings.** It may not seem very important to say "Good morning" to the same people every day or to ask "How was your weekend?" on Monday, but these social pleasantries help make work a nicer place.

- **Mind your manners.** Be considerate of the people around you. Clean up after yourself. Keep your voice down if other people are trying to concentrate. Don't forget to say "Please" and "Thank you."

- **Watch your language.** The words you use reflect on you, for better or worse. Think before you speak. Avoid slang and offensive language. Speak clearly and use correct English. And yes, that includes e-mail!

- **Respond appropriately to questions, compliments, and feedback.** Answer questions to the best of your ability. If you don't know the answer, admit it and promise to find out. If you receive a compliment, don't argue with it. Just say "Thank you." Accept feedback graciously, and remember that its purpose is to help you succeed.

> **Workplace Tip**
>
> If you encounter a co-worker who speaks or behaves in a way that is offensive to you, try to respond in a calm and professional manner. If the problem continues, consult your manager or a Human Resources representative.

Workplace Scenario

You work as a delivery driver and do your job well. Your deliveries are always on time, and you keep good records. However, the other delivery drivers consistently make better tips than you.

1. How might social skills affect your tips? *Social skills could affect how satisfied your customers are with your service and how much they tip.*

2. What are some ways you could try to improve your tips? *Work on exchanging friendly greetings with your customers, speaking clearly and correctly, and saying "Please" and "Thank you."*

Workplace Practice

Jacob works as an administrative assistant at a nonprofit organization. He knows that the director has several important meetings with potential donors lined up for today. Jacob has been told not to interrupt these meetings under any circumstances. While the director is in one of these meetings, another potential donor arrives for her meeting, which is not scheduled to begin for another 20 minutes.

1. How should Jacob greet the potential donor?

2. What would be the best way to handle this situation?

3. If the potential donor asks questions that Jacob cannot answer, what should he do?

Jacob knows how important these meetings are to the director and to the organization, so he should do his best to make the potential donor feel welcome and comfortable. He should greet her in a friendly way, explain that the director is in another meeting, and offer to make the guest comfortable in any way he can. This could include getting her a cup of coffee, glass of water, and/or reading material, or taking her on a tour of the organization. If the potential donor asks questions that Jacob cannot answer, he should admit that he does not know and offer to find out the answers and share them at a later time. Answering incorrectly, even if he is pretty sure he knows the answer, is a risk Jacob should not take in this high-stakes situation.

It's Your Turn!

1. Rita just started a job as a customer service agent for a car dealership. A customer calls and asks her a question about expired warranties, which she did not receive training on yet. How should she respond to the question?

2. You work at a furniture store, and your manager asks you to move a new shipment of chairs to the showroom. The chairs are too heavy to lift by yourself. How should you handle this situation?

3. Your boss asked you to complete a purchasing report while she is out on vacation. You have never completed a purchasing report, but you try to fill it out as best you can. When you show the report to your co-worker, he tells you that you have completed several parts incorrectly.

    A. How should you handle this situation?

    B. When you submit the purchasing report to your boss, she says you did an excellent job. How should you respond?

It's Your Turn! **Answer Key**

1. She should say that she does not know the answer but that she will find someone who can help. She could do this by directing the call to the warranty department.

2. Since you cannot move the chairs on your own, you should ask a co-worker for help. Be sure to ask in a way that is friendly and polite and say "Thank you" afterwards.

3A. You should thank the co-worker for his feedback and ask him how to correct the mistakes. Even though it is disappointing to have your mistakes pointed out to you, it is much better than turning in an incorrect report.

3B. You should thank your boss for the compliment and share the credit with the co-worker who helped you with the report.

Chapter 4 Assessment

Select the best response and the worst response to each situation.

1. You work at the front desk of a hotel, and a guest says he is unhappy with the amount of noise he hears at night. How should you handle this situation?

Best	Worst	
○	○	Excuse yourself to get another co-worker to deal with the problem.
○	○	Apologize for the inconvenience and promise to look into the situation.
○	○	Ask if the guest would like to move to a larger room.
○	○	Tell the guest that hotels are sometimes noisy and he should get over it.

2. You gave a short presentation during a meeting, and you noticed your co-workers looked bored and uninterested. How should you handle this situation?

Best	Worst	
○	○	After the meeting, ask a co-worker to explain why she thinks people were bored by your presentation.
○	○	Decide that you will avoid giving presentations at work from now on.
○	○	Send an angry e-mail to your co-workers criticizing them for ignoring your presentation.
○	○	Go to your supervisor and explain why you do not like giving presentations.

3. Yesterday evening, your manager asked you to close the furniture store where you work. The next day, he tells you that you didn't close the store properly. How should you handle this situation?

Best	Worst	
○	○	Avoid closing the store from now on so that you will not make another mistake.
○	○	Don't bother to ask what you did incorrectly—there's nothing you can do now anyway.
○	○	Tell your manager to have another employee close the store from now on.
○	○	Apologize for the error and ask what you should do next time to close the store properly.

4. You and your co-worker Jax have been assigned to file paid invoices. You complete your part of the job quickly, while your co-worker struggles to finish her part. How should you handle this situation?

Best	Worst	
○	○	Offer to show Jax a quicker way to file the invoices.
○	○	Do something else while Jax files the rest of the invoices.
○	○	Tell your supervisor that Jax works too slowly.
○	○	Tell Jax that she should learn to file faster.

5. Your supervisor has asked you to print out four copies of a 250-page document. You know that other employees need to be able to print documents during this time. How should you handle this situation?

Best	Worst	
○	○	Send the print job to the printer that employees use the least.
○	○	Wait until everyone has gone home for the day to print the copies.
○	○	Send the print job to the main printer in the office.
○	○	Ask the other employees if they need to use the printer for the next two hours.

6. Your co-worker Manny works in the next cubicle. He speaks loudly on the phone and often chats with other co-workers throughout the day. Sometimes he is so loud you have difficulty concentrating on your work. How should you handle this situation?

Best	Worst	
○	○	Tell Manny that his loud talking is very annoying and that he should shut his mouth.
○	○	Complain about Manny's behavior to other co-workers.
○	○	Avoid confronting Manny—you don't want to start an argument.
○	○	Ask Manny politely to lower his voice, and explain that you are having trouble working.

7. At the bakery where you work, your new manager seems annoyed when he interacts with you. How should you handle this situation?

Best	Worst	
○	○	Be overly cheerful whenever you are around your manager.
○	○	Ask your manager if you are doing something to make him displeased with you.
○	○	Don't say anything to your manager and assume it's not personal.
○	○	Ask your co-workers if your manager is nice to them.

8. You work at a small grocery store, and your manager is asking employees to come in next Sunday morning to perform inventory tasks. A family member is getting married that day, so you cannot come to work. How should you handle this situation?

Best	Worst	
○	○	Explain why you can't work that day and offer to make up the time another day.
○	○	Agree to come in to work but call in sick Sunday morning.
○	○	Tell your manager you can't work Sunday mornings.
○	○	Work lots of overtime so that your manager will offer to give you Sunday off.

9. You and two other employees brainstormed ways to increase truck rental sales. Your supervisor wants to have a meeting to discuss everyone's ideas. How should you handle this situation?

Best	Worst	
○	○	Listen to some of your co-workers' ideas, and offer your opinions if a co-worker asks you a question.
○	○	Share your ideas but don't pay any attention when your co-workers share their ideas.
○	○	When a co-worker explains an idea, quickly praise it as a great idea without thinking about it carefully.
○	○	Carefully listen to your co-workers' ideas and consider the pros and cons of each.

Scenario 15

Listen to hear a conversation between a postal delivery driver and his supervisor. You may listen to the conversation more than once before answering the questions.

Active Listening Scenarios are available at www.mysteckvaughn.com/WORK.

10. Which of the following would Will **MOST** likely say to show overall understanding of his manager's words?

    A. "Will I have fewer deliveries next week?"

    B. "Is our office closed this week for the holidays?"

    C. "I'll try to handle the packages more carefully this week."

    D. "I don't know why customers are complaining. I always deliver packages on time."

11. What other information could be relevant to this conversation?

    A. Where the manager will be spending the holidays

    B. The names and credit card numbers of the recipients of the damaged items

    C. The names of the delivery drivers who drive other routes

    D. More tips on how to properly load packages into the delivery truck

12. If Will had said that he has a doctor's appointment next Monday and will need to miss work in the morning, how would his manager **MOST** likely respond?

    A. "Great, I'll see you next Monday morning."

    B. "Thanks for letting me know. I'll schedule another driver for your shift."

    C. "Let me know if any customers complain about damaged items."

    D. "Yes, I'd like to have lunch this week."

For more Chapter 4 assessment questions, please visit www.mysteckvaughn.com/WORK

Check your answers on page 170.

5 Take Responsibility for Learning

Taking responsibility for learning will help you develop your skills and succeed in your career. In this chapter, you will learn about setting appropriate goals and taking initiative in the workplace. You will also practice thinking critically about the signs and graphics you encounter on the job.

Get the Job Done

Essential Tasks

Identify a learning goal

Select and use strategies and information appropriate to learning goal

Monitor/manage progress toward achieving learning goal

Build on What You Know

Setting goals is an essential step toward achieving what you want. Throughout your life, you've probably set lots of goals for yourself. Maybe you've set goals to help you improve your health, goals to help you advance in the workplace, or goals to improve personal relationships or learn a new skill. No matter what types of goals you've set, you've probably learned that setting goals is just the first step in achieving them.

In this lesson, you will learn strategies and skills to help you effectively set and realize goals in the workplace. **Short-term goals** help you manage responsibilities over a short period of time, while **long-term goals** help you improve your performance and attain the career you want. To achieve a long-term goal, you will need to set smaller, short-term goals that help you get there. For example, if you want to become a manager, you may need to take some training courses and prove your skills at a different job first.

In Real Life Training to Achieve

Katherine recently accepted a job as a receptionist at an advertising agency. She is interested in art and advertising, and she hopes to eventually work as a project manager for the company. When she was hired for her current job, her boss was impressed with her ideas and explained that learning new skills and computer programs would help Katherine advance in the company.

Based on her boss's advice, Katherine looked into training sessions to help her learn new computer skills. Unfortunately, the advertising agency offers training for only a few of the computer programs Katherine wants to learn.

 Discuss the following questions with a classmate and share your ideas with the class.

1. What is Katherine's long-term goal?

2. What can Katherine do to help her achieve her long-term goal?

3. How could Katherine learn the computer programs the advertising agency does not offer training for?

Teacher Reminder
Review the teacher lesson at
www.mysteckvaughn.com/WORK

Setting S.M.A.R.T. Goals

Have you ever set a goal that was not reasonable or ended up being too difficult to achieve? Setting the wrong goals can set you up for unnecessary disappointment. You can avoid that by setting goals that are S.M.A.R.T., or *specific*, *measurable*, *attainable*, *realistic*, and *timely*.

- **Specific** What do you hope to accomplish, and why? How are you going to do it?

- **Measurable** How will you know when you have reached your goal? How will you measure your progress toward it?

- **Attainable** Is your goal reasonable, or possible to achieve? What are the steps that will help you achieve your goal?

- **Realistic** Do you have the skills and resources to achieve your goal? Is the goal realistic yet challenging enough that you will feel a sense of accomplishment when you achieve it?

- **Timely** Can you set a concrete time frame to complete your goal? A time limit can motivate you to achieve your goals in a timely fashion.

Think about a short-term or long-term goal you have. Use the questions you read above to help you fill in the following chart and answer the questions. Discuss your responses with the class.

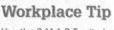

Workplace Tip

Use the S.M.A.R.T. criteria to evaluate your workplace goals. Then make changes as necessary to set goals that will help you achieve your full potential.

Is your goal...	Yes/No	Why or why not?
Specific?		
Measurable?		
Attainable?		
Realistic?		
Timely?		

4. How might you revise your goal to better meet the S.M.A.R.T. criteria?

5. How will you monitor your progress to achieve your goal?

6. Why do you think it's important to set timely goals in the workplace?

Develop Your Skills

Setting goals in the workplace will help you learn new skills, manage your responsibilities, and advance in your company. Practice the following skills to help you set and achieve your goals.

Be S.M.A.R.T.

Whether you are setting short-term or long-term goals, make sure your goals are specific, measurable, attainable, realistic, and timely. Be specific about what you wish to achieve and how you plan to achieve it, and you will succeed in reaching your goals.

> **Examples of goals:**
>
> I want to get a promotion at work. *nonspecific goal*
>
> I will sign up for training sessions at work so I can learn new skills and apply for a promotion. *specific goal*

Once you have set your specific goal, check your goal against the other S.M.A.R.T. criteria. Setting the right goal will go a long way in helping you achieve it.

Change the following nonspecific goals to make them more specific. Discuss your answers with a classmate.

1. I will learn to use a table saw at the construction site.

2. I will be a better customer service representative.

3. I will become the lead cook at the restaurant.

Manage Your Goals

Follow these tips to help you manage and achieve your goals:

- **Develop a plan.** Once you've established a specific goal, develop a plan to help you achieve it. Include in your plan any tasks and deadlines, as well as any resources you'll need to achieve your goal.

- **Monitor your progress.** Create a schedule and keep track of your progress. Adjust your plan or schedule as needed as you work toward achieving your goal.

- **Stay motivated.** It's normal to encounter setbacks when working toward your goal. Keep a positive attitude and make adjustments as necessary to ensure that your reach your goal.

Talk with a classmate about the goal you evaluated on page 131. Discuss your plan for achieving the goal and how you will monitor your progress. Then discuss possible setbacks and how you could overcome them.

> ### Workplace Tip
>
> Having a solid plan can help you achieve almost any goal. Determine what skills you need to learn and what action is required next. Remember, you can set short-term goals to help you work toward your long-term goals.

Break It Down

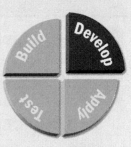

Long-term goals can help you accomplish what you want from your career. A long-term goal might be to complete a big assignment at work or to qualify for a specific position. A long-term goal might also involve a job you hope to hold several years from now.

Long-term goals can seem overwhelming, and you may not know where to start or how to monitor your progress. One helpful strategy is to break down your long-term goal into a few short-term goals that are more manageable. These short-term goals may include taking additional training classes or learning new skills on the job that will help you achieve your long-term goal.

Read the following scenario. Then think about the skills and strategies you've learned as you discuss the questions with a classmate.

Coleman recently started working as a veterinary assistant. He hopes to eventually become a veterinarian. In order to achieve this long-term goal, he will need to attend veterinary school. But for now, he needs to earn money by working full time.

Coleman decides to set some short-term goals that will help him achieve his long-term goal. He has already accomplished one of his short-term goals by applying for a job and becoming a veterinary assistant. He plans to put a certain amount of each paycheck into a special savings account for veterinary school. Coleman's other short-term goals include learning new skills, such as how to weigh animals and take their vital signs, how to explain common medical procedures to pet owners, and how to update records in the computer system.

4. Is Coleman's long-term goal attainable? Why or why not?

5. How could Coleman's short-term goals help him achieve his long-term goal?

6. How else might Coleman benefit from setting short-term goals?

GOT IT?

When you set and work toward your career goals, remember to:

- Ask yourself if the goal is S.M.A.R.T.: specific, manageable, attainable, realistic, and timely.

- Develop a plan, monitor your progress, and stay motivated as you work toward achieving your goal.

- Accomplish long-term goals by breaking them down into more manageable short-term goals.

Answer Key

1. Answers will vary but should include steps one might take to learn to use a table saw.

2. Answers will vary but should include steps one might take to become a better customer service representative.

3. Answers will vary but should include steps one might take to become a lead cook.

4. Yes, Coleman's goal is attainable as long as he follows a plan to achieve each short-term goal.

5. Coleman's skills and experience could help him get into veterinary school. Saving money will also help him pay for school.

6. Achieving his short-term goals will also help Coleman succeed at his current job.

Remember to follow these steps when applying your knowledge:

- ❏ **Set S.M.A.R.T. goals**
- ❏ **Create a plan**
- ❏ **Monitor your progress**
- ❏ **Break long-term goals into short-term goals**

Apply Your Knowledge

Setting and accomplishing your workplace goals requires you to apply different types of skills and strategies in work-related situations.

As you read the following scenarios, think about the skills and strategies you have learned in this lesson. Select what you think is the best response to each situation.

1. You have worked as a host at a restaurant for two years, and you hope to eventually move up to a position in management. One of the managers at your restaurant is moving, and you know his position at the restaurant will open up. In order to be eligible for the position, you must have some management experience or have taken a training seminar for aspiring managers. You don't have the experience, and you haven't taken the seminar. What should you do?

   A. Find out if you can skip the training seminar because you have so much experience as a restaurant host.

   B. Apply for the position when it opens and tell the hiring manager you have completed the seminar, even though you haven't.

   C. Enroll in the training seminar so you can learn the skills you will need and be eligible for the position.

   D. Wait for another job opportunity that doesn't require you to participate in a training seminar.

Best Answer		Worst Answer	

2. You work as a carpenter, and your supervisor has asked you to manage a team on an upcoming project. You have one month to complete the project, and it is your job to make sure you have the people and tools you need to complete it. You are worried because you already have a lot of responsibilities at work. However, you see this as a good opportunity to show your supervisor that you can manage a team and still complete your normal job responsibilities. What should you do?

   A. Create a schedule with small project goals throughout the month to make sure you finish the job on time.

   B. Make managing the team your first priority and try to finish your other responsibilities on the side.

   C. Tell your team members they will need to manage their time carefully, and let you know if they fall behind.

   D. Work as hard as you can and trust that the project will get done one way or another.

Best Answer		Worst Answer	

Put Your Skills to Work!

You work at a shop that does custom screen printing and embroidery. A local company has just placed a large order for shirts and hats for an upcoming event. If you are able to fill the order and satisfy the client, the client will continue to work with your company for future events. The event is one week away, and the order is the largest one your shop has ever filled. There are several things your supervisor needs you to do to make sure you meet the deadline. You must make sure you have the supplies you need, help distribute responsibilities among your team, and prioritize which goods should be made first. Although this is a team effort, your supervisor has asked you to take the lead on the job while she handles all the other orders.

Think about the problem you are facing and put your skills to work! What steps can you take to help your company reach its goal? How will you manage all the responsibilities you have been given?

Think About It!

What skills do you need to practice most to help you reach your workplace goals?

How will you practice these skills?

Setting effective short-term and long-term goals will help you achieve what you want both in and out of the workplace. When you set goals, it is important to make sure your goals are specific, manageable, attainable, realistic, and timely. If your goals meet these criteria, it will be easier to create a good plan, monitor your progress, and accomplish your goal in a timely manner. Remember, though, that obstacles and setbacks may affect your progress. Don't give up! Keep a positive attitude and remain flexible as you work toward getting the job done.

Workplace Tip

When planning how you will manage this situation, remember to think about:

- Setting goals that are specific and achievable.
- Developing a plan, including a schedule or timeline.
- How you will monitor your progress and make sure the project is completed on time.

Answer Key

1. The best answer is C. The best way to qualify for the position is to set a short-term goal to learn the skills required for the position. The worst answer is B. Lying to a manager is never acceptable in the workplace, and without the seminar you will be unprepared for the job.

2. The best answer is A. Creating a schedule will help you manage your responsibilities and monitor your progress as you work toward your goal. The worst answer is D. If you do not make a plan for how the work will get done, you will not be able to monitor your progress and make sure that the project is completed on time.

Test Your WRC Skills

Select the best response and the worst response to each situation.

1. You have just started working as a tile and marble setter. Your boss has asked you to trim several tile pieces and prepare them to be set. You have learned how to use a tile saw to trim down tile pieces, but this is the first time you've been asked to use the saw alone on the job. How should you handle this situation?

Best	Worst	
○	○	Ask a more experienced co-worker to saw the tiles for you.
○	○	Complete the task as your boss has requested and risk breaking the tile saw or injuring yourself.
○	○	Ask a more experienced co-worker to watch as you get started.
○	○	Explain to your boss that you are still getting used to the saw and ask that he assign the task to somebody else.

2. You recently completed your first three months on the job, and your supervisor has called you in to discuss your performance and to offer tips on how you might improve. He would also like you to set learning goals that will help you succeed at your job. How should you determine what kinds of goals to set in this situation?

Best	Worst	
○	○	Ask co-workers what kinds of goals they set and then choose the best from their goals.
○	○	Set goals that will be easy to complete quickly so you can impress your supervisor.
○	○	Ask your supervisor to suggest a few learning goals and then choose from those.
○	○	Set goals based on the tips your supervisor offered on how you might improve.

3. You have taken a new position at a doctor's office. You have been asked to schedule appointments while the head receptionist is away. You have been trained to manage the doctor's schedule, but this is the first time you have had to do it by yourself. How should you handle this situation?

Best	Worst	
○	○	Ask the head receptionist for a quick review before she leaves.
○	○	Do the best you can with what you remember from the training.
○	○	Ask a co-worker to schedule any appointments for you.
○	○	Look for any notes you may have taken from the training.

4. Your supervisor asks you to operate the forklift during your shift. He and your co-workers rely on you to operate the forklift carefully and follow safety guidelines. You are nervous because this is the first time you have operated the forklift outside of training. How should you handle this situation?

Best	Worst	
○	○	Tell your supervisor that someone else should operate the forklift until you've completed more training.
○	○	Ask if a co-worker can help you at the beginning of your shift in case you have questions.
○	○	Explain that you cannot operate the forklift and resign from your position at the warehouse.
○	○	Complete the job as you have been instructed, using what you remember from training to help you.

5. You are having a difficult time with a new computer program you need to use in order to complete your job correctly. How should you handle this situation?

Best	Worst	
○	○	Ask an experienced co-worker for tips and consult the manual to help you learn how to use the program.
○	○	Skip over any tasks that require you to use computer programs you are unfamiliar with.
○	○	Complain to your co-workers about the new computer program and ask them if they have had trouble with it.
○	○	Apply for a different job that does not require you to use this computer program.

6. You are an assistant childcare worker at a day care center. A position with better pay has opened up, and you would like to apply for it. To qualify for the position, you must have an advanced first-aid certification. You have not taken the course necessary to receive this certification. How should you handle this situation?

Best	Worst	
○	○	Wait for a position to open that doesn't require any additional certification.
○	○	Apply for the job and say you have already completed the first-aid certification course, even though you haven't.
○	○	Find out if you can skip the certification because you have so much experience as an assistant.
○	○	Sign up for the certification course so you can qualify for the position.

Check your answers on page 171.

Active Listening

Build on What You Know

In the workplace, setting long-term goals can help you climb the company ladder. But how will you achieve these goals? As you work toward your long-term goals, you will need to set short-term goals to manage each rung on your way up that ladder. Many of those short-term goals will be about learning the skills you need to succeed on the job. Others will be related to managing your job responsibilities. How do you know which goals will help you succeed in the workplace? The first step to setting an effective goal is a simple one: Just open your ears and listen.

When you discuss your job responsibilities with a co-worker or supervisor, you listen to find out what you need to do. You may need to ask questions to understand the task fully or to figure out what you will need to complete it. Listening actively in these situations will help you set the appropriate goals to get the job done. It will also help you understand how your goals fit in with those of your co-workers to support the overall goals of your workplace.

Develop Your Skills

These steps can help you become a better active listener, which will help you set effective goals in the workplace.

- **Listen** for the main idea of the conversation.
- **Confirm** comprehension by using your own words to restate or summarize what you heard.
- **Think** about whether the information you heard confirms or contradicts the information you already know.
- **Ask** questions to clarify any information that isn't clear.

Role-play the following situation. Then discuss the questions.

A new position has opened up at your workplace. Your supervisor **says:** *I've been impressed with your hard work and dedication, and I think this new position is a good fit for you. But there are a lot of applicants for the job. Taking some training classes might improve your chances.*

1. What is your supervisor advising you to do?

2. If you want the new position, what short-term goal may help you get the job?

Workplace Tip

Pay attention to information that helps you know what action to take next. You can then set goals to help you plan for and manage your responsibilities.

Develop Your Skills **Answer Key**

1. Your supervisor thinks you should apply for the position and take some training classes to improve your chances of getting it.

2. Setting a goal of taking and doing well in the training classes may help you achieve your goal of getting the new position.

Apply Your Knowledge

Read the following scenario and answer the questions.

You are in a team meeting to plan for an upcoming construction job. Your supervisor says: *This is an important job for our company, and we need to make sure we complete it on time. On previous jobs, we've sometimes been short on tools and resources. I want each of you to make sure you have what you need to do your job. Because this project is so big, I also need you to pay attention to your progress. If we require more people or supplies, I expect to hear from you before it's too late. Remember, if we're able to finish this job on time, there will be a nice bonus for each of us.*

3. Why did your supervisor call this meeting?

4. What information tells you what action is required of you?

5. What short-term goals might you set to help you manage your responsibilities?

6. What potential reward will you earn if you're able to achieve your goals?

Test Your WRC Skills Scenario 17

Listen to hear a conversation between two co-workers. You may listen to the conversation more than once before answering the question.

Active Listening Scenarios are available at www.mysteckvaughn.com/WORK.

What is the MOST likely reason Grant would consider taking classes at the community college?

A. If he takes the classes, he is sure to get the job in the budget office.

B. He has a hard time in his current job and must improve his math skills.

C. Maria says he will never advance if he doesn't learn new skills.

D. He wants to improve his chances of moving up in the company.

Check your answer on page 171.

Check your answer on page 171.

***Apply Your Knowledge* Answer Key**

3. To prepare employees for an important upcoming job

4. Your supervisor says you must make sure you have the tools and resources you need, monitor your progress on the job, and report any problems before it is too late to resolve them.

5. Answers will vary but should indicate that short-term goals can be set to help monitor progress on the job, manage resources, and complete work in a timely fashion.

6. A bonus

Take Initiative in the Workplace

Build on What You Know

Can you think of a time when you've taken charge of a situation? Maybe you noticed someone who needed help, and you volunteered to assist her or him. Maybe you came up with a plan to fix a problem in your home. Or maybe you saw an interesting job posting and decided to sign up for a class to learn the skills you needed. Taking charge is a valuable skill both in and out of the workplace.

One mistake people often make when they are new in the workplace is waiting to be told what to do. Effective employees know not to do this. Instead, they **take initiative** to do their jobs well. When you take initiative, you think about what needs to be done and do it before being asked. You don't just do the work you are assigned; you also volunteer to help with other tasks. You solve problems creatively, ask for and offer help when it is needed, and seek out opportunities to learn. Taking initiative in the workplace will help you not just meet but exceed expectations. And in doing so, you will build a successful career.

In Real Life   A Job Done Right

Luis works as a cook for a catering company. He and his co-workers are working overtime to fill a large order. His newest co-worker, Barry, is having a hard time with the dish he is working on. He keeps under-cooking or over-cooking it. He can't seem to get it right. The catering team is frustrated by Barry's progress, and everyone is afraid of falling behind. Luis has experience cooking the dish and knows a few tricks to help Barry get it right.

Discuss the following questions with a classmate. Then share your ideas with the class.

1. How could Barry take initiative to improve the situation?

2. How could Luis take initiative to improve the situation?

3. What do you think would happen if nobody took any initiative to improve this situation?

Proactive vs. Passive

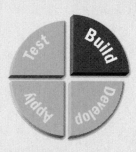

In Lesson 8, you learned that successful team players are proactive rather than passive. There is a strong connection between being proactive and taking initiative in the workplace. When you are proactive, you identify what needs to be done and do it. A passive employee, on the other hand, waits to be told what to do. Proactive employees seek help when necessary and offer help when they identify it is needed. They take initiative to solve problems and succeed in the workplace.

Read the scenarios and identify whether each is an example of *proactive* or *passive* behavior. If the behavior is *passive*, discuss how the employee could take initiative in the situation.

> Damon notices his co-worker is having trouble moving a large box. He pretends not to notice because he also has several packages to load onto the truck.

> Margaret sees a job posting she likes, but she wants to improve her computer skills before applying. She signs up for a weekend computer training seminar at the community college.

> Helen notices the concession lines are getting very long. She decides to take her lunch break and hopes things will slow down by the time she gets back to work at the concession stand.

> The painting company Jason works for has started using a new paint gun. Jason skips the training session and decides he can figure out how to use the paint gun during the next job or just have a co-worker show him how to use it.

Tips for Taking Initiative in the Workplace

Keep the following tips in mind to help you be more proactive and take initiative in the workplace.

- **Recognize early when help is needed.** Ask for help when you need it, and volunteer to help when you think a co-worker could use assistance.

- **Decide what you need and communicate it.** If you require more tools, people, time, or other resources to manage your responsibilities, communicate your needs.

- **Take risks in expressing your opinions.** If you have ideas that might help you and your co-workers, keeping them to yourself won't help anyone. Speak up!

- **Set learning goals.** You will sometimes need to learn new skills to help you succeed at your job. Think about the ways you learn best, and take advantage of opportunities to learn new skills.

- **Volunteer for assignments.** Take on additional responsibilities when you can. This will help you accomplish more and stand out at work.

Develop Your Skills

In this book, you have already learned a lot about solving problems, working well with a team, and taking responsibility for your own learning. Taking initiative will help you do all of these things and excel at your job.

Take Initiative to Solve Problems

When you encounter a problem in the workplace, what do you do? Do you assume someone else will solve it? Do you report it to a supervisor? Effective employees take initiative to solve problems, including asking for help when necessary. The more you learn about your job responsibilities, the better equipped you are to effectively solve problems at work.

You've already learned skills and strategies to help you develop solutions to problems in the workplace. However, knowing problem-solving skills is just the first step. You must take initiative and put your skills to work.

Read the following scenario. Then answer the questions that follow.

Theresa works as a busser at a restaurant. She recently overheard two customers complaining about the overall cleanliness of the restaurant. She decided to follow up by reviewing customer comment cards, and she noticed other customers have complained about the cleanliness of the restaurant's lobby, tables, floors, and restroom.

1. How did Theresa take initiative in this situation?

2. How might Theresa work toward solving the problem without causing conflict with her co-workers?

Take Initiative to Be a Team Player

You've already learned that an effective team player is flexible, respectful of others' ideas, and works hard to achieve group goals. When working with a team, it's crucial that you take initiative to communicate openly and to recognize and resolve conflicts within the team.

Read the following scenario and discuss the questions with a classmate.

Josh's team is installing hardwood floors in a new house. He observes two co-workers arguing. It seems his newest co-worker is holding up the project because he doesn't have much experience cutting the wood panels to the correct length. He has more experience installing the flooring, which is the job Josh is currently doing.

3. What could Josh do to help resolve this conflict?

4. What might happen if Josh did nothing?

Workplace Tip

When working toward solutions to problems in the workplace, remember to:

- Identify the root causes of the problem.
- Seek input from others.
- Communicate your ideas in a way that is courteous and tactful.
- Choose a solution that will deliver the best results for the most people.

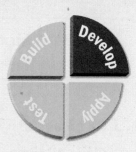

Take Initiative to Learn

No matter what your job is, you'll notice things sometimes change. New computer software may be introduced. New tools and machines might be necessary to complete your job. Maybe a new position opens up, and you are interested in applying for a promotion. To manage your responsibilities and achieve your goals, it is necessary to take initiative to learn new skills.

There are many ways you can learn new skills. Companies often hold training sessions. Community colleges offer courses that might be helpful. Operating manuals or online tutorials can teach you to use computers, tools, and machines. Think about what would help you learn most effectively, and then make a plan to achieve your learning goal. If the online tutorial does not teach you what you need to know, make a new plan. Keep working at it until you have reached your goal.

Read the following scenario. Then answer the questions with a classmate.

Cassandra works as a pharmacist's assistant. One of her responsibilities is keeping track of the pharmacy's inventory and placing orders when new products are needed. The pharmacy recently purchased computers with new software to manage orders and keep track of inventory. Cassandra does not know how to use the new computer software.

    5. How should Cassandra take initiative in this situation?

    6. What might happen if Cassandra does not take action?

Go Beyond Expectations

You've learned how to take personal responsibility in the workplace to ensure that you effectively manage your responsibilities, work well with others, solve problems, and reach your goals. Each day at work gives you a new opportunity to stand out from the crowd. Your value as an employee will be measured by your willingness to take initiative and go beyond what is expected of you. How will you rise to the challenge?

GOT IT?	**Taking initiative is a key to success in the workplace. You are taking initiative when you:**

- Do what needs to be done without being asked.

- Identify a problem and work toward a solution.

- Prevent and resolve conflicts in your workplace.

- Set learning goals and work toward them effectively.

Answer Key

1. She acted on what she heard and reviewed the customer comment cards.

2. Theresa should communicate with her manager and co-workers about the problem in a way that avoids blame. She can work with them to find possible solutions.

3. Josh could offer to switch roles with his co-worker or show him how to cut the flooring more efficiently.

4. If Josh did nothing, his co-workers would continue to argue, and the project may be delayed further.

5. Cassandra should take steps to learn the new computer software.

6. She would have a hard time completing her work and may lose her job.

To-Do List

Remember to follow these steps when applying your knowledge:

❏ **Be proactive**

❏ **Find solutions**

❏ **Resolve conflicts**

❏ **Learn effectively**

Apply Your Knowledge

Solving situational judgment problems requires you to take initiative and apply the skills you have learned to work-related situations.

As you read the following scenarios, think about the different strategies and tips for taking initiative that you have learned in this lesson. Select what you think is the best response and the worst response to each situation.

1. You recently started an on-the-job training program to become a dental assistant. Along with interacting with patients and helping the dentists manage their schedules, you are expected to learn about many different types of dental tools and equipment. You're not sure what many of the machines and tools are called, and you don't know what most of them are used for. What should you do?

    A. Ask one of the dentists to show you how to use each tool and machine.

    B. Watch an online video that shows someone using similar equipment.

    C. Attend the training sessions offered during your on-the-job training.

    D. Observe the dentists working whenever possible.

Best Answer	

Worst Answer	

2. You recently started working as a receptionist for a large corporation. You have basic computer skills but are interested in additional computer training. You believe this training would help you do your job, and you feel that other people at your company would benefit from the training as well. You would like for your employer to provide resources for this training. What should you do

    A. Ask your employer what kinds of training benefits are available to you and your co-workers.

    B. Wait to see if you receive any announcements that classes are being offered through the company.

    C. Practice your computer skills at work when you are not busy with your job responsibilities.

    D. Register for a class at a community college and send your class bills to your employer.

Best Answer	

Worst Answer	

Put Your Skills to Work!

You work as a mail carrier for the post office. It's the holiday season, and work is very busy for everyone at the post office. One of your co-workers has come down with a virus and won't be able to work at all this week. Unfortunately, resources are stretched thin and there is nobody available to cover his shift and route. It is up to you and your co-workers to make sure his route gets covered and that the mail is delivered. Your co-workers are arguing about the best way to split up the route and responsibilities.

> **Think about the problem you are facing and put your skills to work! How can you work with the other mail carriers to manage the extra work? How will you take initiative in this situation?**

Workplace Tip

When solving problems with your work team, be sure to think about:

- What resources you will need.
- How best to utilize your team.
- Your co-workers' input.
- A solution that works for everyone.

Think About It!

What can you do to become a more proactive employee?

How do you think taking initiative might be rewarded?

A common mistake to make in the workplace is to wait for someone else to tell you what to do. Whether you work mostly alone or as part of a team, you should think creatively and independently to identify ways to achieve your personal goals while helping your company or work team achieve its goals. When you take initiative, you take responsibility for identifying tasks you can complete, helping to solve problems, asking for or offering help when necessary, and learning new skills. Learning to take initiative will help you exceed expectations in your current workplace and build a successful career for years to come.

Answer Key

1. The best answer is C. Because this is on-the-job training, there will be training sessions available to help you learn. The worst answer is B. You need to learn about the equipment in your office, and watching an online video about similar equipment will not be as effective as any of the other answer choices.

2. The best answer is A. Being proactive and asking about training opportunities shows your employer that you are interested in learning additional skills that will help the company. The worst answer is D. While your employer may agree to help you get training not offered by the company, it is unprofessional to send your employer a bill having them pre-approve the cost.

Test Your WRC Skills

Select the best response and the worst response to each situation.

1. You work on a manufacturing assembly team, and your new job assignment will require you to use a new machine. You have never used this machine before. How should you handle this situation?

Best	Worst	
○	○	Attend a training session offered by your company.
○	○	Ask your supervisor to show you how to use the machine.
○	○	Watch a video about how the machine was made.
○	○	Observe a co-worker using the machine and take notes.

2. Your company provides a catalog and videos to help employees learn about the products it sells. Every few months, all call center employees have to take a test on the products in the catalog. The next test is one week away. How should you handle this situation?

Best	Worst	
○	○	Ask your supervisor to tell you which products will be on the test.
○	○	Take the test and use your best judgment when choosing answers.
○	○	Read and study any materials your company provides.
○	○	Ask your co-workers to tell you about the products in the catalog.

3. You have taken a job as an electrician's assistant. You don't have much experience with some of the tools you will be required to use, and you'd like to take a training class. You would like for your employer to provide this training, since it would help you do your job. How should you handle this situation?

Best	Worst	
○	○	Keep an eye on the company bulletin board for training opportunities.
○	○	Don't ask about training and just learn what you can on the job.
○	○	See what you can find out about the tools from your co-workers.
○	○	Ask your boss if the company offers any training courses.

4. You are taking a bookkeeping course to improve your workplace skills. You recently received your first grade in the course, and you did not do very well. You feel upset and discouraged. How should you handle this situation?

Best	Worst	
○	○	Drop the class, since you are obviously never going to do well in it.
○	○	Ask your instructor if a study group or any other help is available.
○	○	Don't change anything, but decide to try harder on the next exam.
○	○	Complain to your instructor that the test was too hard.

5. You work as a cook at a popular restaurant, and the management just added a new item to the menu. You have never made this dish before. How should you handle this situation?

Best	Worst	
○	○	Read the description and think of steps you might take to prepare the dish.
○	○	Wait until a customer orders that item and ask someone else to prepare it for you.
○	○	Ask someone with experience making the new dish to teach you how to make it.
○	○	Watch a cooking show that tells how to prepare the dish.

6. Your supervisor has asked you and a co-worker to sand the floors of a house your company is remodeling. The work involves using a large floor sander for the large areas and a smaller hand-held sander for the edges. You and your co-worker decide you will take turns using the large floor sander. You have never used this equipment before, so your co-worker shows you how to use it. However, as soon as you begin using it, something doesn't seem right. How should you handle this situation?

Best	Worst	
○	○	Ask your co-worker what you are doing wrong and how you can improve.
○	○	Keep going and trust that you will get the hang of it with practice.
○	○	Ask your supervisor to assign you to a different remodeling task.
○	○	Turn off the floor sander and make your co-worker finish the task.

Check your answers on page 172.

Identify unstated messages (e.g., overtime, compensatory time, dress code, sick days, lateness, enforced festivities) in company policy statements

Act on information and ideas to meet your purpose (e.g., answer questions, ask questions, make a decision, follow a procedure, complete an assignment, develop healthy relationships)

Consult other resources (people, notes, manuals, etc.)

Workplace Tip

Taking initiative based on faulty or mistaken information can be worse than taking no initiative at all. Be sure you understand the situation completely before deciding what you should do.

Develop Your Skills Answer Key

1. He is frustrated, does not understand the computer program, and is worried about falling behind.

2. You could offer to help your co-worker with the computer program.

Active Listening

Build on What You Know

Have you ever taken the initiative to help a family member without having been asked? What made you decide to help, and how did your family member react? In all likelihood, you heard something that helped you make an **inference** that your help was needed or would be appreciated.

Your ability to take initiative based on inferences you make is also important in the workplace. Making inferences about the underlying meaning or purpose behind a message will help you understand the unspoken rules or expectations of your workplace. It can also help you know when to take initiative to help a co-worker or solve a problem.

Develop Your Skills

When you make inferences about a message you hear, you are identifying the unstated message behind it. These unstated messages often have to do with the purpose of the message, the situation in which it occurs, or the feelings, attitudes, or expectations of the person speaking. Use the following strategies to identify unstated messages in the workplace:

- **Ask yourself questions.** "Why is this person telling me this?" "How does this affect me?" "How does this fit with what I already know?" These questions can help you identify unstated messages.

- **Clarify the message.** Restate, summarize, and ask questions to clarify the speaker's message. Make sure you understand before taking action.

- **Take initiative.** Think about what you learned and determine what action you should take. If you still have questions, find out more information by checking with other people or written sources.

Role-play the following situation with a classmate. Complete your role-play by discussing the following questions.

You stop by a co-worker's office to check his progress on a project you are working on together. He is having problems with a computer program that you know well. He says: *This program doesn't make any sense, and I'm not getting anything done. I'll never finish my work at this rate.*

1. What are some unstated messages behind your co-worker's message?

2. How could you take initiative to improve this situation?

Apply Your Knowledge

Read the following scenario and answer the questions.

You have worked at your company for less than a year, and your supervisor has called a meeting to announce an upcoming work event. She says: *I just want to remind everyone that this Saturday afternoon is our annual Employee Appreciation Picnic. There will be plenty of activities for adults and children, and I'm looking forward to seeing all of your families again this year. As usual, we'll also be handing out awards to celebrate your hard work and contributions. The company will be providing the main courses and beverages for the picnic, but please feel free to sign up if you'd like to contribute sides or desserts. I look forward to seeing you Saturday! And remember, you are welcome to take Monday off as an added "thanks" for attending.*

3. What is the purpose of this announcement?

4. What important expectations are hinted at but not directly stated in the announcement?

5. If you can't attend the picnic for some reason, should you still plan to take Monday off?

Test Your WRC Skills Scenario 18

Listen to hear an explanation of a company policy on family leave. You may listen to the recording more than once before answering the question.

Active Listening Scenarios are available at www.mysteckvaughn.com/WORK.

Based on the family leave policy, which of the following would be the BEST thing to do if you are planning to take family leave?

A. Check the company's vacation policy to find out if you will continue to earn vacation days while on family leave.

B. As soon as possible, begin saving up sick days and vacation days to extend your leave.

C. Work with your supervisor to schedule your leave and plan how to cover your work responsibilities.

D. Send your manager an e-mail with the dates you wish to take your leave and any other relevant details.

Check your answer on page 172.

To-Do List

Remember to follow these steps when applying your knowledge:

❑ **Ask yourself questions**

❑ **Clarify the message**

❑ **Take initiative**

Apply Your Knowledge **Answer Key**

3. To announce the annual company picnic

4. All employees and their families are expected to attend the picnic. Employees are also expected to sign up to bring a food item.

5. No, because the day off is a gesture to thank employees who attend the picnic.

Skills for the Workplace

Inferences

Most signs are designed to give you the most important information in a way that is quick and easy to read. Think about the signs you see on the road. A speed limit sign has only two words and a number on it, but it tells you much more than that. For example, you know that the purpose of the sign is to keep drivers, bicyclists, and pedestrians safe on the road. You can also conclude that the speed posted is in miles per hour and that if you go faster than that, you may get a speeding ticket.

At work, some signs you see may show important safety information, while others may explain company policies. Since the information on a sign is often limited to just a few words and **visuals**, it may not tell you absolutely everything you need to know. To understand the signs you encounter in the workplace, you will often need to make inferences, or go beyond the stated message, to understand the unstated purpose or meaning.

Workplace Scenario

The dress code at SGB Industries is business-casual. Refer to the guidelines below for appropriate workplace attire.

Allowed	Not Allowed
· Collared shirts	· T-shirts
· Ladies' blouses	· Blue jeans
· Sweaters	· Shorts
· Dress pants or cotton trousers	· Sneakers
· Skirts (knee length or longer)	· Flip-flops
· Dress shoes or boots	· Revealing clothing
	· Dirty or ripped clothing

1. What kind of dress code does this workplace have? *Business-casual*

2. What clues on the sign help you understand the dress code? *The picture shows an example, and the chart lists acceptable and unacceptable clothing.*

3. Why might this sign have been posted? *Some people may have been wearing inappropriate clothing to work.*

Workplace Practice

You see the following sign on the wall near a manufacturing assembly line:

1. Is it acceptable to use your cell phone while working on the assembly line?

2. Why do you think cell phone use is prohibited on the assembly line?

It is not acceptable to use your cell phone while working on the assembly line. This is because you could get hurt if you aren't paying attention.

> ### Workplace Tip
> When you start a new job, look for signs and important notices around your workplace. If you don't understand something you see on a sign, ask your manager to explain what it means.

It's Your Turn!

1. Jo works at MQ Electronics. His sister stops by to give Jo his lunch and sees this sign on the door. Why do you think MQ Electronics has this rule

   > Visitors of MQ Electronics MUST wear a temporary security badge and be escorted by an employee at all times. **No exceptions!**

2. You work at a construction site and see this sign posted in several places. What is the purpose of this sign?

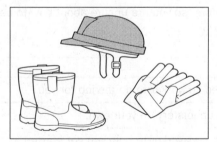

3. Rashonda has knocked over a barrel of a chemical solution. She gets some paper towels and is about to start cleaning up the solution when she sees this sign. How should Rashonda handle this situation?

   > **SAFETY FIRST!** In case of a chemical spill, evacuate the area and alert your manager. **DO NOT** attempt to clean the spill.

It's Your Turn! Answer Key

1. Possible answer: This rule prevents unauthorized people from being on company premises, which helps to keep the company's employees and products safe.

2. The purpose is to keep workers safe by informing them about safety gear that must be worn at the construction site.

3. She should evacuate the area and alert her manager.

Chapter 5 Assessment

Select the best response and the worst response to each situation.

1. The restaurant where you work recently installed a new payment processing system. You have never used this system before. How should you handle this situation?

Best	Worst	
○	○	Use the system to figure out how it works.
○	○	Ask another co-worker to explain how to use the system.
○	○	Go online and read about the system.
○	○	Attend a training session to learn the system.

2. You work as a telemarketer. You know a little Spanish, but you feel that knowing Spanish fluently would be helpful in some situations. How should you handle this situation?

Best	Worst	
○	○	When you call a Spanish speaker, transfer him or her to a co-worker who knows Spanish better than you.
○	○	Find a Spanish conversation club to join after working hours.
○	○	Continue to do your work, and avoid calls to Spanish speakers because you don't speak the language fluently.
○	○	Ask your supervisor if he or she will teach you Spanish.

3. Your supervisor asks you to remove the upholstery from a bed frame. You have never removed upholstery from a bed frame before, so you are unsure about how to begin. How should you handle this situation?

Best	Worst	
○	○	Ask an experienced co-worker to do the job for you.
○	○	Try to remove the upholstery on your own.
○	○	Ask an experienced co-worker to help you get started.
○	○	Ask your supervisor to find someone else to do it.

4. Your boss has asked you to come up with three work-related skills to learn over the next six months. At the end of six months, your boss will evaluate your progress. How should you handle this situation?

Best	Worst	
○	○	Pick three skills now but wait until later to learn them so that you appear to make a lot of progress quickly.
○	○	Tell your boss that you don't need to learn any new skills because you already do your job fine.
○	○	Pick three skills that would be easy for you to master so that you can impress your boss.
○	○	Pick three skills that would most help you at your job, and focus on mastering one skill every two months.

5. Your manager wants to produce a training manual for new employees in your office. The manual would include instructions on how to perform common tasks and how to use office equipment. He asks you for advice on what to include in the manual. How should you handle this situation?

Best	Worst	
○	○	Think about what you had to learn when you first started at the office, and advise your manager to include training for those skills.
○	○	Tell your manager that new employees will probably need a training session on the company's various policies.
○	○	Explain to your manager that you don't remember what you had to learn to complete your job, and he should ask a newer employee.
○	○	Tell your manager that when you first started at the office, you had a lot of problems understanding certain computer programs.

6. The company where you work hangs the following sign in the break room. You see a co-worker throw a bag of aluminum cans in the garbage can. How should you handle this situation?

Best	Worst	
○	○	Tell your co-worker it's bad for the environment to throw away aluminum cans and that he should be more considerate.
○	○	Go tell your supervisor about your co-worker's behavior.
○	○	Point to the sign and politely remind your co-worker that recycling helps the environment.
○	○	When your co-worker leaves, move the cans into the proper recycling bin.

7. You work as an usher at a theater. The following sign hangs on the ticket station.

You've noticed one of your co-workers has been letting her friends into the theater even though they do not have tickets. How should you handle this situation?

Best	Worst	
○	○	Point to the sign and kindly remind your co-worker of the ticket policy.
○	○	Tell your co-worker that if she doesn't stop letting her friends in, you'll tell the theater owner.
○	○	Start letting your friends in for free, too—if your co-worker does it, why can't you?
○	○	Start ignoring your co-worker so she knows you are upset with her.

8. You work as a data entry clerk at a hospital. Your supervisor has asked all data entry clerks to aim to type 55 words per minute. You average about 30 words per minute. How should you handle this situation?

Best	Worst	
○	○	Apply for another job that does not require fast typing skills.
○	○	Ask a co-worker who types faster than you do to teach you how to type faster.
○	○	Practice typing faster at home for a few hours each week.
○	○	Keep working as usual and hope that your supervisor doesn't notice you falling behind.

9. You work as a customer service representative for an Internet service provider, and you would like more training on how to deal with technical support issues. You believe you can help customers with minor technical issues. How should you handle this situation?

Best	Worst	
○	○	Check to see what technical support training is available.
○	○	Ask an employee in technical support to give a demonstration of how to provide technical support.
○	○	Tell your supervisor you want to learn more technical support skills or you're quitting.
○	○	Practice helping customers with technical support issues.

Scenario 19

Listen to hear a conversation between an employee and his manager. You may listen to the conversation more than once before answering the questions.

Active Listening Scenarios are available at www.mysteckvaughn.com/WORK.

10. If Jason wants to know if he's being too loud when he makes calls in the office, how might he find out?

    A. By looking in the company's employee handbook

    B. By asking his wife when he talks to her on the phone

    C. By recording his phone calls and listening back

    D. By asking his co-workers if he is bothering them

11. Based on this conversation, how could Jason be more courteous to his co-workers?

    A. He could come to work late so he can talk to his wife more before work.

    B. He could have phone conversations at his desk only in the mornings.

    C. He could have phone conversations outside during his lunch break.

    D. He could send his wife text messages throughout the day while at work.

12. Why do you think Jason's supervisor, not his co-workers, had this conversation with him?

    A. Because only Jason's supervisor cares if he talks loudly on the phone

    B. Because Jason's co-workers were not comfortable bringing the issue to his attention

    C. Because Jason's supervisor wanted to know what Jason was saying on the phone

    D. Because Jason's co-workers don't like him and didn't want to talk to him

Check your answers on page 173.

For more Chapter 5 assessment questions, please visit www.mysteckvaughn.com/WORK

WorkSkills™ Glossary

The following words were used in the *WorkSkills™* Situational Judgment and Active Listening book. Knowing these words will help you as you study for the National Work Readiness Credential assessment.

A

accusations (ak-yoo-**zey**-shuhnz) claims that someone has done something wrong

active listening (**ak**-tiv **lis**-uhn-ing) listening closely to what speakers say and how they say it in order to understand their full message

B

best solution (best suh-**loo**-shuhn) the solution from a group of possible solutions that gets the best results for the most people

brainstorming (**breyn**-stawr-ming) the process of generating ideas

C

clue words (kloo wurdz) words and phrases that help you understand what something you read or hear is about or relates to

communication barriers (kuh-myoo-ni-**key**-shuhn **bar**-ee-erz) issues that stand in the way of effective communication, such as the lack of a common language

compromise (**kom**-pruh-mahyz) to give up some of what you want to reach an agreement

conflict (**kon**-flikt) a disagreement or opposition of people's interests or ideas

conflict resolution (**kon**-flikt rez-uh-**loo**-shuhn) the process of solving a disagreement in a peaceful way

cooperate (koh-**op**-uh-reyt) to work together to achieve a common aim

courteous (**kur**-tee-uhs) being polite and considerate of others

D

decision making (dih-**sizh**-uhn **mey**-king) the process of choosing the best option out of the options available

F

formal setting (**fawr**-muhl **set**-ing) a setting that requires professional interaction and behavior

I

"I" messages (ahy **mes**-ij-ez) messages that use the word "I" instead of "you" to express your feelings about a situation; meant to avoid blaming or attacking the other person or people

inference (**in**-fer-uhns) a thought or idea concluded from available information and prior knowledge

informal setting (in-**fawr**-muhl **set**-ing) a setting that is friendly, casual, and relaxed

interpersonal skills (in-ter-**pur**-suh-nl skilz) the skills you need to interact and communicate with others in a respectful and productive way

L

long-term goals (**lawng**-turm gohlz) goals you set to achieve or help you manage responsibilities over a long period of time

N

"negative" voice (**neg**-uh-tiv vois) a way of speaking to yourself that is unhelpful and discouraging

negotiate (ni-**goh**-shee-eyt) working with others to find a solution that can be agreed upon

nonverbal cues (non-**vur**-buhl kyooz) ways people communicate without using words, such as facial expressions, hand gestures, body language, and eye contact

O

objectively (uhb-**jek**-tiv-lee) not being influenced by personal feelings or biases

P

passive (**pas**-iv) waiting to be told what to do; not taking action or thinking ahead

"positive" voice (**poz**-i-tiv vois) a way of speaking to yourself that is kind and encouraging

proactive (proh-**ak**-tiv) thinking ahead and taking action to get things done

problem analysis (**prob**-luhm uh-**nal**-uh-sis) examining and defining a problem to find its solution

problem-solving skills (**prob**-luhm **solv**-ing skilz) skills that use your knowledge to identify a problem and outline ways to solve it

pros and cons (prohz and konz) reasons for and against something

R

relevant (**rel**-uh-vuhnt) connected in a sensible or logical way

resistance (ri-**zis**-tuhns) something or someone that opposes or disagrees with something or someone

root causes (root **kawz**-ez) the reasons or factors that cause a problem

S

self-talk (**self**-tawk) what you say to yourself in your head; your inner voice

short-term goals (**shohrt**-turm gohlz) goals you set to achieve or help you manage responsibilities over a short period of time

social cues (**soh**-shuhl kyooz) signals that listeners can identify to understand the important points of a conversation

social skills (**soh**-shuhl skilz) the personal skills you need to get along with others in social and workplace situations

summarize (**suhm**-uh-rahyz) to repeat, in your own words, something you read or hear

T

tactful (**takt**-fuhl) being respectful of another person's feelings or point of view

take initiative (teyk ih-**nish**-ee-uh-tiv) to think and act creatively and proactively to complete tasks, help others, and learn new skills

team players (teem **pley**-erz) members of a team who help the team achieve common goals and who want everybody on the team to succeed

V

verbal cues (**vur**-buhl kyooz) words or phrases you can use to indicate you understand what someone is saying

visuals (**vizh**-oo-uhlz) images, such as graphics or pictures, used to show or explain something

Answers and Explanations

Lesson 1 Test Your WRC Skills (pages 24–25)

1. The best answer is *Apologize and tell the customer you will take care of it right away*.
This is the best answer because you acknowledge the customer's problem and say you will take immediate action to solve it. **The worst answer is *Calmly explain that the restrooms are not your problem*.** This is the worst answer because although you are remaining calm, you make no attempt to address the customer's problem.

2. The best answer is *Remove the broken toys and ask how you should dispose of them*.
This is the best answer because you have identified the problem that the broken toys could be dangerous, and you choose a course of action that keeps the children safe. **The worst answer is *Tell the toddlers that they should not use the broken toys*.** This is the worst answer because you are responsible for the toddlers' care, and they may be hurt by the dangerous toys.

3. The best answer is *Explain the error to your manager and ask her to add your name*.
This is the best answer because you have identified the reason for the problem and have taken the appropriate action to correct the mistake. **The worst answer is *Do nothing and hope that your manager will correct the mistake*.** This is the worst answer because it does not address the problem. If your name is not on the list, you cannot do what your manager requested, which is for each employee to sign up for a one-hour time slot.

4. The best answer is *Explain the accident to your supervisor and ask how to proceed*.
This is the best answer because you are addressing the problem in a productive and honest way. This problem has probably happened before, and your supervisor will know what to do to fix the machine. **The worst answer is *Tell your supervisor that another employee broke the wheel*.** This is the worst answer because lying about the accident does not address the problem, and being dishonest can lead to problems in the future.

5. The best answer is *Apologize for the inconvenience and offer the customer an approved discount for special orders*.
This is the best answer because it acknowledges the customer's frustration about having to wait for a special order and offers him a solution that improves the situation. **The worst answer is *Tell the customer that if he is unhappy with your shop, he should take his business elsewhere*.** This is the worst answer because it does not help solve the customer's problem, and it is also poor customer service.

6. The best answer is *Check the other supply rooms for safety goggles*.
This is the best answer because you are taking the necessary steps to solve the problem and following your factory's safety policy. **The worst answer is *Don't wear eye protection, and be extra careful in your area*.** This is the worst answer because it ignores the problem, is a violation of company policy, and could be dangerous.

Lesson 2 Test Your WRC Skills (pages 32–33)

1. The best answer is *Check with your supervisor to see if it is safe to work, and trust that he will keep you and the client informed of the situation.*
This is the best answer because it is your supervisor's responsibility, not yours, to decide when you should stop working and to keep the client aware of the situation. **The worst answer is *Continue working despite the potential danger because it is important to keep the client happy.*** This is the worst answer because you should never put yourself in danger unnecessarily.

2. The best answer is *Find a workshop to take.*
This is the best answer because it is the first step in the plan toward improving your speaking skills. **The worst answer is *Practice speaking to a friend.*** This is the worst answer because it does not help you complete your plan.

3. The best answer is *Explain your policy and ask that he take only one sample.*
This is the best answer because you are following the plan that you made to solve the problem of running out of samples. **The worst answer is *Tell the customer that he is being selfish and doesn't need three samples.*** This is the worst answer because it is insulting to the customer, especially since he was not already informed about the policy.

4. The best answer is *Explain why you made the schedule and offer the employee the option of filling in for employees who need to miss a shift.*
This is the best answer because you explain to the employee the reason for the new schedule and provide a way for her to make extra money if she needs to. **The worst answer is *Give the employee more hours by taking away another employee's hours.*** This is the worst answer because it creates an imbalance in the schedule, which was the original problem you were trying to solve.

5. The best answer is *Check job postings for a mail carrier position.*
This is the next step because you must find an open position before you can apply, accept, and begin a new job. **The worst answer is *Begin work as a mail carrier.*** This is the worst answer because you must complete several steps before you can begin the new job.

6. The best answer is *Explain that you need to refill the printer, and quickly get a spare paper roll from another counter.*
This is the best answer because you explain the problem to the customer and then quickly work to solve it. **The worst answer is *Close your register and direct the customers to other checkout lines.*** This is the worst answer because the other lines are already long and closing your line will cause stress on both co-workers and customers. Furthermore, the problem of refilling the printer does not get solved.

Chapter 1 Assessment
(pages 36–39)

1. The best answer is *Tell the parent you understand her concern and that you'll speak with your supervisor about the snacks.*
This is the best answer because you acknowledge the parent's problem and express that you will take action to solve it. **The worst answer is** *Tell the parent you'll look into providing snacks with less sugar, but then don't do anything.* This is the worst answer because you are reassuring the parent you will address the problem, but you make no attempt to follow through.

2. The best answer is *Remind your co-workers that wearing goggles and gloves will help them avoid getting injured.*
This is the best answer because you have identified the root cause of your co-workers' problem and offered helpful information to help them solve their problem. **The worst answer is** *Don't do anything because it's not your problem.* This is the worst answer because injuries are not something that you and your co-workers should ignore.

3. The best answer is *Talk to the clerk about the problem and ask if he needs help getting the mail out on time.*
This is the best answer because you are addressing the root cause of the late mailings and offering to help find a possible solution to the problem. **The worst answer is** *Assure the client that the packages were sent on time even though you know they weren't.* This is the worst answer because it does not address the problem. The client will be even more upset if she finds out you are lying, and you haven't offered any solutions to solve the problem.

4. The best answer is *Immediately tell your supervisor and offer to correct your mistake.*
This is the best answer because you address the root cause of the problem in an honest and responsible way. By offering to fix the labels and re-file the records, you are generating a possible solution. **The worst answer is** *Don't do anything and hope no one notices your mistake.* This is the worst answer because you are not addressing the problem or providing a solution. Furthermore, you could cause disruptions in service to the patients.

5. The best answer is *Talk to the office manager about possible ways to implement a recycling program in the office.*
This is the best answer because you are choosing the option that is most likely to get you the results you want and is also appropriate for your workplace. **The worst answer is** *Tell your supervisor that his attitude is environmentally irresponsible.* This is the worst answer because insulting your supervisor is not appropriate for the workplace and will not help you succeed in solving the problem.

6. The best answer is *Point to the sign and explain why the elevator shouldn't be used.*
This is the best answer because you have helped your co-worker interpret and understand the sign and follow the safety procedures correctly. **The worst answer is** *Get on the elevator with your co-worker because there is no actual fire.* This is the worst answer because during a fire drill, employees should behave as if there were an actual fire. By taking the elevator, you are disobeying safety procedures.

7. The best answer is *Enroll in a Web design course at your local community college.*
This is the best answer because this is the most effective way to learn Web design. Once you complete the course, you will be more likely to be considered for positions in the communications department. **The worst answer is** *Learn Web design during work hours using a company computer.* This is the worst answer because you should spend work hours fulfilling the responsibilities of your current job, not using company equipment to learn what you need to know for a different job. This is not the most effective way to learn Web design, and you risk getting in trouble for violating company policies.

8. The best answer is *Kindly explain to your co-worker why it is important to not let food spoil.*
This is the best answer because you have planned and implemented your solution in order to fix the problem. **The worst answer is** *Let your co-worker keep messing up so she gets fired.* This is the worst answer because this does not offer a solution to the problem. Your co-worker will continue to make mistakes until she gets fired, which will cause you to be short an employee in the cafeteria.

9. The best answer is *Politely interrupt your co-worker and explain why people need to be quiet near the operating room.*
This is the best answer because explaining why it is important to be quiet in this area will prevent a disturbance in the operating room. **The worst answer is** *Don't do anything—you don't want to interrupt his phone call.* This is the worst answer because it is more important to keep the area outside the operating room quiet than to not disturb the co-worker's call. The people in the operating room need quiet in order to prevent injuries to the patient.

10. The best answer is *Explain the reasons why all employees should wash their hands after using the restroom.*
This is the best answer because you are analyzing the information on the sign to help your co-worker understand the reasons why employees should wash their hands. **The worst answer is** *Immediately tell your manager to fire your co-worker for disobeying the hand-washing policy.* This is the worst answer because trying to get your co-worker fired does not address the problem effectively and could cause even more problems.

11. The best answer is *Offer to help gather the materials before traveling to high schools.*
This is the best answer because you are addressing the root cause of the problem and being helpful to your manager. **The worst answer is** *Don't do anything—it's your manager's problem, not yours.* This is the worst answer because you are making the problem worse by not helping your manager address the root cause of the problem. Furthermore, the problem affects your work performance as well. It is in your best interest to find a solution.

12. The best answer is *Talk to your supervisor to discuss taking time off to see a doctor.*
This is the best answer because you are choosing an option that will most likely solve your sleep problems and is appropriate to your workplace. **The worst answer is** *Ignore how tired you are and keep driving your scheduled routes.* This is the worst answer because this plan does not offer a solution to your problem. You could cause an accident if you drive while tired, so it is important to address your sleeping issues.

Lesson 3 Test Your WRC Skills (pages 48–49)

1. C. Ask for approval before working any more overtime hours.
Option C is correct. Susan tells Ben to notify her or another supervisor about overtime he wishes to work. Option A is incorrect because Susan tells Ben his commitment and hard work have not been overlooked. Option B is incorrect because Susan does not ask Ben to work more overtime. Option D is incorrect because Susan is concerned about the overtime policy, not with how Ben spends his weekend.

2. B. Ben is not as strong of a worker when he's worked too many hours.
Option B is correct. Susan points out specifically that Ben is not as strong an employee when he works too many hours. Option A is incorrect because Susan's job is to make sure Ben does his job properly, not to make sure he enjoys his time off. Option C is incorrect because Susan never mentions how many hours other employees work. Option D is incorrect because the scenario does not state that either of these things occurred.

3. D. To help the company and the employees succeed
Option D is correct because Susan mentions that policies are in place for the good of the company and to help employees succeed. Option A is incorrect because Susan doesn't mention that policies assure that jobs are completed on time. Option B is incorrect because the answer refers only to the overtime policy. Option C is incorrect because Susan doesn't mention that the policies encourage workers to take on more responsibilities.

4. A. He will follow company policies.
Option A is correct. The purpose of the meeting was to make sure Ben follows company policies, such as the overtime policy. Option B is incorrect because, while Ben should complete his work on time, it is not the focus of the meeting. Option C is incorrect because Ben is not asked to stop working overtime. Option D is incorrect because Ben needs to follow company policies, not memorize them word for word.

5. B. To welcome new employees and describe their responsibilities
Option B is correct. The speech is for an orientation meeting to welcome new employees and tell them what they need to do. Option A is incorrect because it addresses two small points from the meeting, not the meeting's purpose. Option C is incorrect because employees are not asked any questions. Option D is incorrect because the speaker does not read through any company policies; she asks employees to read them carefully.

6. D. Read the orientation documents.
Option D is correct. The speaker explains that the orientation documents will tell employees more about their responsibilities. Option A is incorrect because the employees have not yet begun training. Option B is incorrect because the speaker does not mention that the policies will tell employees about their responsibilities. Option C is incorrect because the employees are not advised to set up an appointment with the dentist.

7. A. So they can help keep the office running smoothly
Option A is correct. The speaker specifically mentions that knowing the basics will help employees keep the busy office running smoothly. Option B is incorrect because the employees are not preparing to be dentists; they are preparing to be dental assistants. Option C is incorrect because employees are not asked to assist one another during training. Option D is incorrect because understanding orientation documents precedes basic training.

8. C. Some of the dental assistants' duties will be difficult to learn, but help will be available.
Option C is correct. The speaker says that some duties may take months to learn, but that employees should ask for assistance when necessary. Option A is incorrect because the speaker doesn't mention the option of repeating the program. Option B is incorrect because the speaker points out that some duties will be difficult to learn. Option D is incorrect because the speaker doesn't mention whether some employees will not make it through the training process.

Lesson 4 Test Your WRC Skills (pages 56–57)

1. B. One week to finish presentation
Option B is correct. It is important for Kati to remember she has just one week to finish the VPN presentation. Option A is incorrect because Jack does not ask Kati to report back in a few weeks. Option C is incorrect because nothing in the conversation suggests that Kati's children need to arrive late to school. Option D is incorrect because this is not the most important information to remember.

2. A. She should ask, "Can you please explain what you mean by 'back on track'?"
Option A is correct. Kati should ask for clarification if she does not understand a phrase. Option B is incorrect because Kati should not wait until later to clarify Jack's message. Option C is incorrect because that language is unprofessional and won't help Kati better understand Jack. Option D is incorrect because it's important that Kati understand everything Jack says.

3. C. Stop letting things slip at work and go back to being an excellent employee.
Option C is correct because before she let things slip at work, Jack says Kati was an excellent employee. Option A is incorrect because Jack doesn't advise Kati to take a leave of absence. Option B is incorrect because Jack has not asked Kati for apologies; he has asked her to get back on track. Option D is incorrect because it is clear that Kati was once able to manage her responsibilities before she started letting things slip.

4. D. She says, "I won't let you or the company down."
Option D is correct. By saying this, Kati shows she has understood what Jack has asked of her. Option A is incorrect because Kati says this before Jack has shared his message. Option B is incorrect because apologizing does not show that Kati knows what action is necessary. Option C is incorrect because it doesn't show that Kati will improve her work performance.

5. C. First-time job seekers
Option C is correct. The recording specifically says that Smart Start is designed for first-time job applicants. Option A is incorrect because WEB has another program for workers affected by cutbacks and layoffs. Option B is incorrect because the Single Parent Connection is the program designed to help single parents. Option D is incorrect because currently employed individuals do not require Smart Start.

6. B. Smart Start, prep for interview
Option B is correct. A first-time job seeker would most likely be interested in Smart Start. Option A is incorrect because it does not note information that would be important for a first-time job seeker to remember. Option C is incorrect because this is the name of a program for single parents. Option D is incorrect because a first-time job seeker would not have experience with layoffs.

7. D. Access the career center's Web site.
Option D is correct. The recording instructs people who are unable to hold to visit the center's Web site. Option A is incorrect because if you need the information now, calling back another time won't help you. Option B is incorrect because there's no way to track down others who have used the center. Option C is incorrect because depending on what time it is, you may not be able to visit the center.

8. A. Childcare services
Option A is correct. Childcare services are necessary for a single parent seeking work. Options B, C, and D are incorrect because childcare is essential for single parents seeking work and would be a higher priority than getting assistance with a job application, connecting with other job-seekers, or finding assistance with writing a résumé.

Chapter 2 Assessment (pages 60–61)

1. D. So you have instructions available in case you need to reset your password in the future

Option D is correct. Taking notes will help you remember how to reset the password in case you need to in the future. Options A and C are incorrect because in this situation, being polite and practicing note-taking skills are not the main purpose of taking notes about resetting your password. Option B is incorrect because the technician is teaching you a skill, not training you to do his job.

2. C. Tell the client when you think you can send him the completed bid.

Option C is correct. The client wants to know approximately what time you think you will send the bid. When you estimate the time of arrival, you are giving a realistic time of completion. Option A is incorrect because the client has called because he expects a bid from you. Option B is incorrect because the client is asking how long it will take to complete the bid, not the project. Option D is incorrect because if you promise to send the bid in an hour and don't, the client will lose trust in your company.

3. A. From now on, try to leave your house ten minutes earlier each morning.

Option A is correct. If you leave your house ten minutes earlier, you will avoid being late and keep your job in good standing. Options B and C are incorrect because both leaving work 15 minutes early and continuing to arrive at work late could cause you to lose your job. Option D is incorrect because telling your supervisor when other employees are late does not address your own tardiness.

4. B. Start sending complaints to the resolution department.

Option B is correct. Although you were trained to send complaints to your supervisor, you should follow your department manager's directions and start sending them to the resolution department. Option A is incorrect because the department manager has probably informed your supervisor about the change already. Option C is incorrect because if you keep sending complaints to your direct supervisor, you will be disobeying the new directions. Option D is incorrect because saying this is disrespectful and will damage your relationship with your department manager.

5. D. The employee should attend the session again if he or she wants to review safety and sanitation practices.

Option D is correct. Although the employee is not required to attend the session, it might be a good chance to review safety and sanitation practices. Options A and B are incorrect because according to the speaker, an employee who has already attended a session in the past is not required to do so again. Option C is incorrect because learning new skills, not setting an example, is an appropriate reason to attend a training session.

6. A. Kitchen manager

Option A is correct. The speaker is most likely a kitchen manager because a kitchen manager's job is to ensure that all employees are properly trained in safety and sanitation practices. Options B, C, and D are incorrect because cooks, waiters, and dishwashers do not have the responsibility of training employees in safety and sanitation.

7. C. "Could you please tell me what *pathogens* are?"

Option C is correct. This is the most courteous and effective way to find out what an unfamiliar word means. Option A is incorrect because this is not a courteous or effective way of learning the unfamiliar word. Option B is incorrect because it does not request the meaning of the unfamiliar word. Option D is incorrect because you should be able to understand the general purpose of the training session based on the speaker's words. This option also has nothing to do with discovering the meaning of the word.

Lesson 5 Test Your WRC Skills (pages 70–71)

1. The best answer is *Ask Alex to refill the copy machine if he uses all the paper*.
This is the best answer because you recognize and define the conflict in a calm, constructive way. **The worst answer is** *Tell your supervisor that Alex never refills the copy machine's paper*. This is the worst answer because you are making an accusation about Alex instead of defining and restating the conflict.

2. The best answer is *Stop Paul and explain why it is unsafe for uncertified workers to operate forklifts.*
This is the best answer because you have identified the problem that uncertified workers driving forklifts could be dangerous. You have also taken immediate action and restated the conflict in a calm way without assigning blame. **The worst answer is** *Tell Paul to drive the forklift slowly and carefully so he can avoid accidents.* This is the worst answer because it ignores the conflict, condones a dangerous behavior, and goes against your supervisor's orders.

3. The best answer is *Explain to your co-worker that she could get in trouble for using her work phone and computer to apply for other jobs.*
This is the best answer because you have acknowledged the conflict and used details to restate the conflict in a helpful way. **The worst answer is** *Do nothing and hope that your manager catches your co-worker while she is looking up other jobs.* This is the worst answer because you are not acknowledging the conflict or taking effective steps to resolve it.

4. The best answer is *Calmly explain the policy and point out the sign.*
This is the best answer because you acknowledge the conflict calmly and take steps to resolve it. **The worst answer is** *Tell the customer not to come back to the deli again.* This is the worst answer because it does not attempt to define or resolve the conflict, and it may cost the deli a customer.

5. The best answer is *Kindly ask your manager to close his door when he makes calls.*
This is the best answer because you are using a calm and rational approach to acknowledge the conflict. It is likely that the manager does not realize the problem and will help you resolve it. **The worst answer is** *Slam your manager's door shut whenever he is being loud.* This is the worst answer because you make no attempt to define or restate the conflict, and slamming the door will only make the conflict worse.

6. The best answer is *Apologize for the error and tell the patient that you will correct the charges on her bill.*
This is the best answer because you identify an area of agreement with the customer and take action to resolve the conflict. **The worst answer is** *Inform the patient there is nothing you can do and hang up the phone.* This is the worst answer because you do nothing to address the patient's complaint or improve the situation. Also, hanging up the phone is rude and will escalate the conflict.

Lesson 5 Active Listening
Test Your WRC Skills (page 73)

B. Do some tasks but not others
Option B is correct. This sentence in the scenario provides the context needed to determine the meaning of the phrase "cut corners": "You can't *cut corners* to save time, or we could have some serious safety issues on our hands." Option A is incorrect because saving energy is not a topic mentioned in the conversation. Option C is incorrect because *cut corners* is a just an expression, and it does not relate in any way to the actual cutting of objects. Option D is incorrect because attending safety training would result in fewer safety issues, not more.

Lesson 6 Test Your WRC Skills (pages 80–81)

1. The best answer is *Explain that you are closing, but the customer can make a quick purchase if she knows what she wants to buy.*
This is the best answer because each party gets something they want: the customer gets to buy her gift, and you get to close the store without staying too late. **The worst answer is *Suggest that the customer look for a gift at another gift shop that is open later.*** This is the worst answer because the customer is inconvenienced, and your shop does not get the customer's business.

2. The best answer is *Suggest that your co-worker use headphones when she listens to the radio at work.*
This is the best answer because you will be able to concentrate, and your co-worker can continue to listen to her music. **The worst answer is *Bring in a radio and play it really loud so your co-worker knows how annoying it is.*** This is the worst answer because it prevents both you and your co-worker from doing work and will most likely escalate the conflict.

3. The best answer is *Ask Roberto to fill in for employees who need their shifts covered.*
This is the best answer because Roberto can make extra money and the other employees do not have to sacrifice their own hours. Furthermore, they have somebody available to cover for them if they need to take time off. **The worst answer is *Give Roberto the extra shifts he needs until he pays off the expenses.*** This is the worst answer because it disregards the other employees' needs completely. It will most likely cause further conflict among you, Roberto, and the other employees.

4. The best answer is *Allow the resident to watch TV in a community room away from the rooms where the other residents sleep.*
This is the best answer because it negotiates a solution that results in both sides getting what they want. **The worst answer is *Alternate between nights the resident can watch TV and nights he can't.*** This is the worst answer because neither side of the conflict gets what they want on a consistent basis, and the conflict is likely to continue.

5. The best answer is *Propose that the drivers split tips equally so that it is in everybody's best interest to make as many deliveries as possible.*
This is the best answer because it offers a win-win solution that will hopefully be more effective than the previous solution. **The worst answer is *Speed on your way to make the deliveries so that you can try to make more deliveries.*** This is the worst answer because you are putting yourself in danger, and it does not resolve the conflict.

6. The best answer is *Ask your supervisor if you can move to a different desk.*
This is the best answer because it resolves the problem and places both you and Jane in an environment where you can get your work done. **The worst answer is *Start reading Jane's e-mail over her shoulder.*** This is the worst answer because you are escalating the conflict and neglecting your work.

Lesson 6 Active Listening
Test Your WRC Skills (page 83)

C. Angry
Option C is correct. The speaker uses his voice to communicate that he is irritated with Malik's behavior. Options A, B, and D are incorrect because they convey emotions other than anger and do not match the speaker's message.

Chapter 3 Assessment
(pages 86–89)

1. The best answer is *Tell your manager that the client's request conflicts with the instructions you were given.*
This is the best answer because you acknowledge the conflict before beginning the job. As a result, your manager can consult with the client or advise you on what to do next. **The worst answer is *Tell your manager that you won't do the job because you don't like the client's attitude.*** This is the worst answer because you are refusing to do what you were hired for, and you have insulted the client, which is never a good idea.

2. The best answer is *Confront the attendant and tell him that you know the job is stressful but he should always be respectful.*
This is the best answer because you are agreeing that the job is stressful but informing the co-worker that he must be respectful to the residents. **The worst answer is *Ignore the behavior and hope that it will eventually stop or that a supervisor will talk to the attendant.*** This is the worst answer because you are not acknowledging the conflict in any way.

3. The best answer is *Tell your manager why you think the schedule is causing the problem.*
This is the best answer because you are giving your manager important details that could help resolve the conflict. **The worst answer is *Reschedule the cleaning staff without consulting with your manager*.** This is the worst answer because it will escalate the disagreement between you and your manager.

4. The best answer is *Call Mery and let her know that she needs to get a doctor's note to prove she is sick.*
This is the best answer because you are helping Mery by telling her what she needs to do to keep her job, and you are helping your supervisor by providing the proof that Mery is sick. **The worst answer is *Don't contact Mery—it's her responsibility to get the doctor's note on her own.*** This is the worst answer because Mery could get fired unjustly, and your supervisor would have to begin looking for a replacement, which can be difficult.

5. The best answer is *Order the more expensive pens for the employees who want them and the cheaper pens for everyone else.*
This is the best answer because this solution satisfies the people who want the more expensive pens and still helps to keep costs down for the company. **The worst answer is *Tell the staff to bring their own pens because you don't want to deal with the problem.*** This is the worst answer because this solution does not satisfy either party involved in the conflict.

6. The best answer is *Suggest that Eric and Sara keep a log of who cleans large messes and when.*
This is the best answer because you have offered a fair method of monitoring the cleaning so no one does more work than the other. **The worst answer is *Tell your manager that Eric and Sara are fighting about who should clean up messes.*** This is the worst answer because you have not offered a solution that can be monitored for effectiveness and fairness. Furthermore, you are involving the manager in a fairly insignificant issue.

7. The best answer is *Analyze the contractor's strengths and experience and try to match him with a project that fits his abilities.*
This is the best answer because matching the contractor with a project that fits his strengths and experience benefits both him and your company. This agreement is likely to produce the best results for the most people. **The worst answer is *Assign the contractor to the project anyway and hope he picks the skills up as he goes along.*** This is the worst answer because the contractor is not qualified for the project. This decision would cause the client to be disappointed with the results, which would harm both your company's and the contractor's reputations.

8. The best answer is *Point to the sign and explain to Travis that he could slip and hurt himself.*
This is the best answer because when you observe that Travis does not comprehend the meaning of the sign, you help him understand why the sign is important to his safety. **The worst answer is *Don't stop Travis because he should know not to run in this area.*** This is the worst answer because Travis could be injured if he slips. A responsible employee will work to help others follow safety rules.

9. The best answer is *Ask the two employees nicely if they could work a little late to help stock the merchandise.*
This is the best answer because you are courteously asking your co-workers to help resolve the conflict. This is the option that is likely to help you get the best results for the most people. **The worst answer is *Call the merchandise company and yell at them for sending the shipment late in the day.*** This is the worst answer because you could put your company's relationship with the supplier in jeopardy. Furthermore, yelling at the company does not help resolve the conflict.

10. D. Using a company computer to shop online is against company policy.
Option D is correct. The speaker tells Karen that she cannot shop online at work because it is against company policy. This is the main idea of what the speaker says. Option A is incorrect because the speaker did not talk about sending personal e-mails. Options B and C are incorrect because it against company policy to shop online using company computers.

11. B. Friendly but firm
Option B is correct. The speaker is telling Karen about the computer policy in a polite manner, but she is firm in her explanation of the policy. Options A, C, and D are incorrect because the speaker is not overly cheerful, bored and uninterested, or aggressive and hostile while explaining the policy.

12. B. "Can you explain why the policy states that employees can't shop online?"
Option B is correct. If Karen did not understand the policy, she would ask for clarification about why she cannot shop online. Options A and C are incorrect because Karen is not trying to clear up confusion about the company policy. Option D is incorrect because lunch breaks are not related to the topic of the conversation.

Lesson 7 Test Your WRC Skills
(pages 98–99)

1. The best answer is *As you redo the work, show the new co-worker how to measure correctly.*
This is the best answer because you are being cooperative by helping to fix an error made by someone else. Also, you offer clear input to help your co-worker understand how to do his job. **The worst answer is** *Tell the new co-worker that he messed up and he better not do it again.* This is the worst answer because it is not friendly or tactful, and it does not help your co-worker understand what he did wrong or how to correct it.

2. The best answer is *Calmly explain that you do not mind making the copies, but his requests this week have been excessive.*
This is the best answer because the copies need to be made, but the administrative assistant also needs to know that you expect him to fulfill his job duties. Communicating this clearly and tactfully is the best approach to the issue. **The worst answer is** *Tell the administrative assistant that he is needs to get his act together and then hang up the phone.* This is the worst answer because it is disrespectful to the co-worker. While it is understandable that you would be frustrated by the situation, your response is not tactful, and you risk damaging your relationship.

3. The best answer is *Tell the customer that you will go get a supervisor who can help her.*
This is the best answer because you are helping a customer even though your shift is over. This is a positive and courteous behavior that helps create a cooperative workplace. **The worst answer is** *Ignore the customer and clock out for the day.* This is the worst answer because you do nothing to assist the customer or improve the situation. You are not being cooperative to the customer or to your co-workers who could use the help.

4. The best answer is *Ask your co-worker to send all personal e-mails to your home computer.*
This is the best answer because asking your co-worker to send the videos and pictures to your home computer is a tactful way to resolve the situation. **The worst answer is** *Ask your co-worker to keep the news about her baby to herself.* This is the worst answer because it is not friendly or tactful, and will probably offend your co-worker.

5. The best answer is *Offer to help the co-worker when he returns from the job site.*
This is the best answer because Kyle is offering help and is being courteous even though he is in a rush. **The worst answer is** *Wave his hands to indicate that he is in a rush and can't stop to help.* This is the worst answer because it is not a friendly or courteous way to react to a new co-worker's request for help.

6. The best answer is *Go talk to Holly to ask if there is a problem, and see if she needs help with something.*
This is the best answer because it is a friendly, courteous way to address the situation. Also, asking if a co-worker needs help promotes cooperation on the assembly line. **The worst answer is** *Yell at Holly to speed things up because her work is slowing down the entire assembly line.* This is the worst answer because yelling at a co-worker is rude, disrespectful, and not at all helpful.

Lesson 7 Active Listening
Test Your WRC Skills (page 101)

C. "Does anyone have any questions about the handout?"
Option C is correct. At the end of the scenario, the speaker distributes a handout and asks everyone to review it. It makes sense that the next thing the speaker would say would be to ask if there are any questions about the handout. Option A is incorrect because the speaker just asked everyone to take a look at the handout. Also, the phrase "no further questions" does not make sense because no questions have been asked yet. Option B is incorrect because the speaker never mentions hazardous waste. Option D is incorrect because "I look forward to seeing you at the job site next week" indicates the end of the meeting, but it is clear from the scenario that the meeting is not over.

Lesson 8 Test Your WRC Skills (pages 108–109)

1. The best answer is *Begin clearing the tables and preparing for the midday rush.*
This is the best answer because you are being a proactive member of the staff. You are evaluating what needs to be done and taking action to complete the task without being asked. **The worst answer is** *Take a long break because there is nothing to do.* This is the worst answer because you should always assume that there is something that you can be doing. If you aren't sure what to do, ask your supervisor.

2. The best answer is *Thoroughly prepare the car well before the customer arrives.*
This is the best answer because you are being dependable. You are following through on your responsibility in a thorough and timely manner. **The worst answer is** *Decide not to prepare the car because there are other cars in the lot that the customer could rent.* This is the worst answer because you are failing to complete the task requested of you and, thus, showing that you are an unreliable member of the team.

3. The best answer is *Apologize for the error and work with the family to find a suitable, available room.*
This is the best answer because you are adapting to the circumstances, taking responsibility, and attempting to solve the problem. **The worst answer is** *Tell the family that your co-worker is always messing up, and now there's nothing you can do to help them.* This is the worst answer because you are not being a good teammate to your co-worker or helping the family. Complaining about your co-worker to the hotel guests is not being a good team player. It is your job to help the guests, regardless of whether or not a co-worker made a mistake.

4. The best answer is *Offer to stop for a few minutes so that she can complete her task.*
This is the best answer because you are adjusting your actions to meet the needs of others. **The worst answer is** *Tell her to wait until tomorrow since your job is more important.* This is the worst answer because you are not treating your co-worker with respect, and your lack of flexibility does not contribute to the overall success of the crew.

5. The best answer is *Walk over to the ladder and steady it yourself.*
This is the best answer because you are taking action to help another worker. **The worst answer is** *Don't do anything and hope that Modesto doesn't hurt himself.* This is the worst answer because you are not doing anything to prevent a potentially dangerous situation. If Modesto were to get hurt, you would feel terrible, and the ability of the team to complete the job would suffer.

6. The best answer is *Place the patient on hold and quickly ask a co-worker to show you how to transfer the call.*
This is the best answer because you are seeking help from another member of the team so that the patient's call is transferred quickly and correctly. **The worst answer is** *Tell the patient on the phone that she will have to call back when the other receptionist is working.* This is the worst answer because you are not being proactive to complete the task at hand.

Lesson 8 Active Listening
Test Your WRC Skills (page 111)

D. "I'll buff the floors while Sylvia cleans the tables and chairs."
Option D is correct. The cleaning-crew member repeats the assigned tasks back to the supervisor to show that he understands and will divide those tasks between himself and another team member. Option A is not correct because the supervisor did not ask the cleaning crew to clean out the storage room but to clean specific items *in* the storage room. Option B is incorrect because although buffing the floor is mentioned in the meeting, information about the floor buffer is unrelated to the supervisor's request. Option C is incorrect because setting up the sound system is the responsibility of the maintenance crew, not the cleaning crew.

Lesson 9 Test Your WRC Skills (pages 118–119)

1. The best answer is *Request a supervisor.*
This is the best answer because a supervisor will likely have more experience dealing with dissatisfied customers and will be best equipped to help you diffuse the conflict. **The worst answer is *Quit your job.*** This is the worst answer because quitting your job doesn't solve the problem with the customer, and you are left unemployed.

2. The best answer is *Talk to your supervisor to see if a mistake was made.*
This is the best answer because speaking with your supervisor and pointing out the oversight will likely help you solve the problem. **The worst answer is *Take a co-worker's computer and printer.*** This is the worst answer because taking a co-worker's computer creates a new problem and may cost you your job.

3. The best answer is *Talk with Sarah when she is calm, and ask her if something was said that upset her.*
This is the best answer because talking to Sarah while she is upset will likely make her feel even more overwhelmed. Waiting until she is calm before discussing the matter will produce a better outcome and help you solve the problem. **The worst answer is *Contact Sarah's supervisor to discuss her behavior during training.*** This is the worst answer because you should try to find out what the problem is before involving Sarah's supervisor.

4. The best answer is *Tell Ms. Donato that you want to do well, and ask her to explain things more clearly while you are still learning.*
This is the best answer because expressing that you want to do well but need help learning will show that you are motivated to learn and succeed at your job. Ms. Donato will likely take more time and be more understanding while training you. **The worst answer is *Complain about how unfair and incompetent Ms. Donato is as a supervisor.*** This is the worst answer because complaining about Ms. Donato behind her back will damage your relationship with her and possibly other employees. Doing so doesn't solve your problem, and it may cost you your job.

5. The best answer is *Tell Veronica that because of her talking on the phone, you are having difficulty hearing what the supervisor is saying.*
This is the best answer because Veronica may not realize she's being disruptive. Pointing out the problem and tactfully asking her to quiet down will likely resolve the issue. **The worst answer is *Tell Veronica that she is being her typical rude and loud self, just like everyone says.*** This is the worst answer because aggressively confronting Veronica will damage your working relationship and will also further disrupt the meeting.

6. The best answer is *Talk with your co-worker and request that she not discuss personal matters during the meeting, as it is disruptive.*
This is the best answer because your co-worker may not realize she is disrupting the meeting. Calmly discussing the issue will solve the problem and maintain your working relationship. **The worst answer is *Confront your co-worker during the meeting and loudly inform her that no one cares about her or her personal business.*** This is the worst answer because confronting your co-worker will further disrupt the meeting and will damage your working relationship.

Lesson 9 Active Listening
Test Your WRC Skills (page 121)

C. "Lena, your bonus idea may be just what is needed to boost our customer service."
Option C is correct. Reinforcing Lena's idea may improve her attitude, and doing so also addresses the goal of improving customer service. Option A is incorrect because telling Lena to miss a meeting doesn't solve her problem with Mabel or address the goal of improving customer service. Option B is incorrect because discussing a co-worker's dislike of another co-worker with a supervisor will damage Karl's relationship with the co-worker and will not solve their conflict. Option D is incorrect because questioning Lena's idea at this point will only further discourage her.

Chapter 4 Assessment (pages 124–127)

1. The best answer is *Apologize for the inconvenience and promise to look into the situation.*
This is the best answer because you are acknowledging the guest's problem in a tactful, respectful way and offering a solution to his problem. **The worst answer is *Tell the guest that hotels are sometimes noisy and he should get over it.*** This is the worst answer because you should speak to guests in a tactful and respectful manner. You are also not offering a reasonable solution to the problem.

2. The best answer is *After the meeting, ask a co-worker to explain why she thinks people were bored by your presentation.*
This is the best answer because you are using a strategy to gain input from another person about your presentation. You can use this information to make your next presentation more engaging. **The worst answer is *Send an angry e-mail to your co-workers criticizing them for ignoring your presentation.*** This is the worst answer because you are not using an effective strategy to gain input about your presentation, and sending an angry e-mail to your co-workers is not appropriate workplace behavior.

3. The best answer is *Apologize for the error and ask what you should do next time to close the store properly.*
This is the best answer because this is the most professional and effective way to let your manager know that you are sorry and want to learn how to improve your job performance. **The worst answer is *Don't bother to ask what you did incorrectly—there's nothing you can do now anyway.*** This is the worst answer because if you don't ask your manager what you did wrong, you will make the same mistake the next time you need to close the store.

4. The best answer is *Offer to show Jax a quicker way to file the invoices.*
This is the best answer because when you offer to help someone finish a job, you are adjusting your actions to help everyone succeed. **The worst answer is *Tell your supervisor that Jax works too slowly.*** This is the worst answer because you are not taking into account how you can help Jax improve her performance nor are you helping to accomplish the task. By involving the supervisor, your relationship with Jax may be compromised.

5. The best answer is *Send the print job to the printer that employees use the least.*
This is the best answer because sending a large document to a printer that not many people use allows for employees to use the main printer while you complete the job. You are adjusting your actions to take into account the needs of others and the task you must accomplish. **The worst answer is *Send the print job to the main printer in the office.*** This is the worst answer because you might prevent other employees from using the printer while the large document prints.

6. The best answer is *Ask Manny politely to lower his voice, and explain that you are having trouble working.*
This is the best answer because this is a tactful and friendly way of telling Manny that his loud voice is interrupting your work. **The worst answer is *Tell Manny that his loud talking is very annoying and that he should shut his mouth.*** This is the worst answer because although you have communicated the problem to Manny, you have done so in a rude, tactless manner. This could lead to ill will and a poor working relationship between you and Manny in the future.

7. The best answer is *Ask your manager if you are doing something to make him displeased with you.*
This is the best answer because you are seeking input from your manager in order to understand why he seems annoyed when he interacts with you. **The worst answer is *Don't say anything to your manager and assume it's not personal.*** This is the worst answer because you are not doing anything to improve the situation. Your manager may be unhappy with your job performance or attitude. You should try to find out the reason for your manager's behavior so you can have a more positive relationship with him.

8. The best answer is *Explain why you can't work that day and offer to make up the time another day.*
This is the best answer because you are communicating clearly why you cannot come to work. By offering to make up the time another day, you are showing that you're hardworking and responsible. **The worst answer is *Agree to come in to work but call in sick Sunday morning.*** This is the worst answer because you are acting irresponsibly by lying to your manager and not communicating what you need. Your dishonesty puts your manager in a bad position because he might not be able to find someone to cover for you on short notice.

9. The best answer is *Carefully listen to your co-workers' ideas and consider the pros and cons of each.*
This is the best answer because when you listen carefully to others and think about what they say, you are being courteous and demonstrating respect for their ideas. **The worst answer is *Share your ideas but don't pay any attention when your co-workers share their ideas.*** This is the worst answer because when you don't listen to others, you are showing that you don't care about what they have to say. This behavior is rude and inappropriate in the workplace.

10. C. "I'll try to handle the packages more carefully this week."
Option C is correct. Will is confirming comprehension of what his manager said by paraphrasing his manager's request. The manager requested that Will be more careful when handling boxes and packages. Option A is incorrect because the manager explained that there would be more deliveries next week. Option B is not correct because the manager said that Will will have to make more deliveries because of the holidays. Option D is incorrect because the manager explained that customers complained because of damaged items.

11. D. More tips on how to properly load packages into the delivery truck
Option D is correct. The speaker had been discussing ways to ensure that packages do not get damaged. Additional tips could be helpful to Will. Options A, B, and C are incorrect because none of this information helps Will ensure that packages are delivered undamaged during the holidays.

12. B. "Thanks for letting me know. I'll schedule another driver for your shift."
Option B is correct. If Will said he has an appointment next Monday, his manager would probably try to find another driver to cover his shift. The manager would base his response on the information Will gave him. Option A is incorrect because Will said he could not come to work on Monday morning. Options C and D are incorrect because Will was discussing his appointment, not customer complaints or having lunch this week.

Lesson 10 Test Your WRC Skills (pages 136–137)

1. The best answer is *Ask a more experienced co-worker to watch as you get started.*
This is the best answer because a more experienced co-worker will be able to give you tips and let you know if you are doing anything wrong. **The worst answer is *Complete the task as your boss has requested and risk breaking the saw or injuring yourself.*** This is the worst answer because it is better to ask for help or admit you're not ready to use a tool than to break the tool or risk injury.

2. The best answer is *Set goals based on the tips your supervisor offered on how you might improve.*
This is the best answer because setting learning goals that address areas in which you need to improve will help you become a better employee. **The worst answer is *Set goals that will be easy to complete quickly so you can impress your supervisor.*** This is the worst answer because choosing a goal that will be easy to complete only shows that you don't take the learning goal or improving in your job very seriously.

3. The best answer is *Ask the head receptionist for a quick review before she leaves.*
This is the best answer because the head receptionist will be able to refresh your memory, which will help you complete your task. **The worst answer is *Ask a co-worker to schedule any appointments for you.*** This is the worst answer because you, not your co-worker, have been asked to schedule appointments. This answer suggests you are not interested in learning how to do your job.

4. The best answer is *Ask if a co-worker can help you at the beginning of your shift in case you have questions.*
This is the best answer because having help early in the shift will ensure that you are able to safely perform your job. **The worst answer is *Explain that you cannot operate the forklift and resign your position at the warehouse.*** This is the worst answer because being nervous about a new job is no reason to quit. A little help from an experienced co-worker will help ease your nerves so you can perform your job with confidence.

5. The best answer is *Ask an experienced co-worker for tips and consult the manual to help you learn how to use the program.*
This is the best answer because you will get tips to help you improve immediately, as well a comprehensive overview of the program that will help you perform your job. **The worst answer is *Skip over any tasks that require that you use computer programs you are unfamiliar with.*** This is the worst answer because you will not complete your work, which may cause problems for you and your company.

6. The best answer is *Sign up for the certification course so you can qualify for the position.*
This is the best answer because enrolling in the course will help you reach your goal. **The worst answer is *Apply for the job and say you have already completed the first-aid certification course, even though you haven't.*** This is the worst answer because without the course you will not be qualified to do your job. Furthermore, your lie will jeopardize the safety of the children you care for.

Lesson 10 Active Listening
Test Your WRC Skills (page 139)

D. He wants to improve his chances of moving up in the company.
Option D is correct. Improving at math will help Grant achieve his long-term goal of moving up in the company. Option A is incorrect because Maria doesn't guarantee that Grant will get the job if he takes math classes. Option B is incorrect because Grant's math skills aren't a problem in his current job. Option C is incorrect because Maria never says Grant can't advance without improving his math skills.

Lesson 11 Test Your WRC Skills (pages 146–147)

1. The best answer is *Attend a training session offered by your company.*
This is the best answer because a company training session will show you how your company expects you to operate the machine. **The worst answer is *Watch a video about how the machine was made.*** This is the worst answer because to do your job on the assembly line, you should have hands-on training on the machine. Watching a video about how the machine was made will not tell you everything you need to know to operate the machine safely.

2. The best answer is *Read and study any materials your company provides.*
This is the best answer because reviewing the materials will help you understand your company's products, do well on the test, and learn the information you need to do your job. **The worst answer is *Ask your supervisor to tell you which products will be on the test.*** This is the worst answer because asking your supervisor to tell you what is on the test defeats the purpose of the test and suggests that you are not interested in learning the information needed to do your job well.

3. The best answer is *Ask your boss if the company offers any training courses.*
This is the best answer because you are taking charge of the situation and working effectively toward your learning goal. If you want to take a training class and want your company to provide it, then you should take the initiative to ask about training benefits. **The worst answer is *Don't ask about training and just learn what you can on the job.*** This is the worst answer because you have identified what you need to learn effectively, but this option does not help you accomplish that goal.

4. The best answer is *Ask your instructor if a study group or any other help is available.*
This is the best answer because you are taking responsibility for your learning and asking for what you need to help you succeed. **The worst answer is *Drop the class, since you are obviously never going to do well in it.*** This is the worst answer because giving up will not help you learn new skills or improve in the workplace. You can certainly learn bookkeeping, or any other subject, if you put in the time and effort.

5. The best answer is *Ask someone with experience making the new dish to teach you how to make it.*
This is the best answer because a co-worker or lead chef can show you exactly how your restaurant likes to prepare this particular dish. **The worst answer is *Wait until a customer orders that item and ask someone else to prepare it for you.*** This is the worst answer because learning how to prepare the new dish is part of your job. If you have someone else complete your work, you won't improve your skills, and you may lose your job.

6. The best answer is *Ask your co-worker what you are doing wrong and how you can improve.*
This is the best answer because your co-worker has the experience to teach you what you need to know. Learning to use this equipment will help you complete your assigned task and succeed on the job. **The worst answer is *Turn off the floor sander and make your co-worker finish the task.*** This is the worst answer because learning how to use this equipment will help you succeed on the job. If you refuse to learn how to use it, your job performance will suffer. It is also unfair to your co-worker, who will be forced to do more than his fair share to get the job done.

Lesson 11 Active Listening
Test Your WRC Skills (page 149)

C. Work with your supervisor to schedule your leave and plan how to cover your work responsibilities.
Option C is correct. Taking the initiative to meet with a supervisor as early as possible will help your company manage your responsibilities while you are out. Option A is incorrect because the policy doesn't mention anything about accumulating vacation days while on family leave. Option B is not the best answer because, although you may wish to save up sick days and vacation days to extend your leave, meeting with your supervisor is more important. Option D is incorrect because the policy requires you to meet with your manager to schedule your absence, not inform your manager via e-mail.

Chapter 5 Assessment
(pages 152–155)

1. The best answer is *Attend a training session to learn the system.* This is the best answer because attending a training session would be the most effective way to learn the new system. **The worst answer is** *Use the system to figure out how it works.* This is the worst answer because if you use the system without knowing it well, you may make mistakes that require a lot of work to correct.

2. The best answer is *Find a Spanish conversation club to join after working hours.*
This is the best answer because joining a conversation club will help you reach your learning goal. In a conversation club, you can practice speaking conversational Spanish with others. **The worst answer is** *Continue to do your work, and avoid calls to Spanish speakers because you don't speak the language fluently.* This is the worst answer because you have not done anything to reach your goal of learning more Spanish and you are not doing your job.

3. The best answer is *Ask an experienced co-worker to help you get started.*
This is the best answer because asking an experienced co-worker for help is a good strategy to help you get started with the job. **The worst answer is** *Try to remove the upholstery on your own.* This is the worst answer because you risk damaging the furniture if you don't remove the upholstery properly.

4. The best answer is *Pick three skills that would most help you at your job, and focus on mastering one skill every two months.*
This is the best answer because if you learn the skills over the six-month period, you will have a better chance at mastering them and applying them to your job. **The worst answer is** *Tell your boss that you don't need to learn any new skills because you already do your job fine.* This is the worst answer because you are showing your boss that you are not interested in improving your performance or achieving new learning goals.

5. The best answer is *Think about what you had to learn when you first started at the office, and advise your manager to include training for those skills.*
This is the best answer because you are considering your own experiences to provide useful information to teach a new employee at the office. **The worst answer is** *Explain to your manager that you don't remember what you had to learn to complete your job, and he should ask a newer employee.* This is the worst answer because you aren't making any effort to remember your learning process, and you're not helping your manager achieve his goal (which will probably help you as well).

6. The best answer is *Point to the sign and politely remind your co-worker that recycling helps the environment.*
This is the best answer because you are helping your co-worker understand the sign. You are also helping your company reduce waste and help the environment. **The worst answer is** *Go tell your supervisor about your co-worker's behavior.* This is the worst answer because you haven't solved the problem of your co-worker not understanding the sign. You also risk creating tension with your manager and co-worker over an issue you are capable of solving.

7. The best answer is *Point to the sign and kindly remind your co-worker of the ticket policy.*
This is the best answer because you are reminding your co-worker that it is against company policy to allow anyone into the theater without a ticket. **The worst answer is** *Start letting your friends in for free, too—if your co-worker does it, why can't you?* This is the worst answer because rather than solving the problem, you are joining your co-worker in violating company policy.

8. The best answer is *Practice typing faster at home for a few hours each week.*
This is the best answer because practicing typing at home is a reasonable and effective way to increase your typing speed over time. **The worst answer is** *Keep working as usual and hope that your supervisor doesn't notice you falling behind.* This is the worst answer because this is not an effective way to reach your learning goal, and falling behind may cost you your job.

9. The best answer is *Check to see what technical support training is available.*
This is the best answer because attending a technical support training session would be an effective way to learn how to administer technical support to a customer. **The worst answer is** *Tell your supervisor you want to learn more technical support skills or you're quitting.* This is the worst answer because this is not a courteous or professional way to ask for training.

10. D. By asking his co-workers if he is bothering them
Option D is correct. Jason could get feedback from his co-workers by asking them if his volume is affecting them. Option A is incorrect because the company employee handbook wouldn't offer feedback on how loud Jason is talking. Option B is incorrect because Jason's wife is not in the office when he calls, so she wouldn't know whether he is affecting his co-workers. Option C is incorrect because this is not an effective way of getting feedback on how loud Jason sounds to his co-workers.

11. C. He could have phone conversations outside during his lunch break.
Option C is correct. If Jason wants to keep in touch with his wife and be courteous at the same time, he could have phone conversations with her outside during breaks. Option A is incorrect because if Jason is late for work, he could put his job in jeopardy. Option B is incorrect because he would disturb his co-workers if he had conversations at his desk in the morning. Option D is incorrect because if he sent text messages to his wife throughout the day, he would be violating the spirit of the policy, which is that personal communication should take place outside of work hours.

12. B. Because Jason's co-workers were not comfortable bringing the issue to his attention
Option B is correct. Since Jason's co-workers were not willing to take care of the conflict themselves, Jason's supervisor stepped in to mediate the conflict. Option A is incorrect because Jason's co-workers were the ones who told his supervisor about his loud talking. Option C is not correct because Jason's supervisor never asks Jason about the content of his personal conversations. Option D is incorrect because Jason's co-workers only have a problem with his loud talking. It is unlikely that they dislike him so much that they do not want to talk to him.